OCR
Revise
Psychology

OCR and Heinemann are working together to provide better support for you

Jean Arrick
Sandra Latham
Bryan Saunders
Consultant: Fiona Lintern

Official Publisher Partnership

Heinemann is an imprint of Pearson Education Limited, a company incorporated in England and Wales, having its registered office at Edinburgh Gate, Harlow, Essex, CM20 2JE. Registered company number: 872828

www.heinemann.co.uk
Heinemann is a registered trademark of Pearson Education Limited

Text © Pearson Education Limited 2009

First published 2009

13 12 11 10 09
10 9 8 7 6 5 4 3 2 1

British Library Cataloguing in Publication Data
A catalogue record for this book is available from the British Library

ISBN 978 0 43580 773 3

Edited by Toynbee Editorial Services Ltd
Typeset by Phoenix Photosetting, Chatham, Kent
Cover design by Pearson Education Limited
Cover photo/illustration © iStock Photo
Printed and bound in the UK by Henry Ling

Every effort has been made to contact copyright holders of material reproduced in this book. Any omissions will be rectified in subsequent printings if notice is given to the publishers.

Contents

Introduction

This book has been designed to support your revision for OCR A2 Psychology. It is a revision guide that can be used alongside your OCR A2 Psychology textbook and your own notes made in class. The page references quoted in this guide refer to the OCR A2 Psychology textbook also published by Heinemann. If you have studied other research you can adapt the research-specific worksheets to accommodate these.

How to use this book

This book covers the two A2 units, Options in Applied Psychology, and Approaches and Research Methods in Psychology. For each Unit 3 topic, there is an outline of the four areas you need to know. You can use this as a tick sheet to identify what you need to revise before the exams. There are activities to help you make revision notes of the research covered in Unit 3 and some opportunities to identify issues you may use when you are evaluating research.

 As the research used in Unit 3 can help you in Unit 4 synoptic essays, this symbol has been used to identify places where the activities may be particularly useful for Unit 4.

You may want to complete the activities in pencil as you finish one topic to consolidate your knowledge, and then reuse the book to revise before the exam. One of the important factors in revising is to do something with the material. Psychologists know that semantic processing (working out the meaning) of material helps recall more than just reading or listening to something. So make sure that when you revise you use the material in some way – for example, to make revision cards or mind maps, or to write and answer short questions. Activities such as these will make the research more memorable and so easier to recall in the exam.

After each section of revision or consolidation activities, there is an Exam Café which enables you to summarise the work you need to revise and then shows how this can be applied in the exam using exemplar answers. These will help you to identify best practice in answering exam questions effectively to maximise your marks. Try making up questions which could also appear on the exam paper, and write a high-grade answer for each one. You could pair up with a friend and mark each other's work. The mark scheme is available on the OCR website, www.ocr.org.uk.

Revision tips

- Make sure you have notes on all of the research you will need in the exam (this may include theories, studies, models, approaches/perspectives, debates/issues and methodology).
- Try using colour to co-ordinate your notes, one colour for each topic when you make revision cards – for example, your notes for option 1 on yellow cards, for option 2 on blue cards, issues on green cards and research methods on pink cards.
- Use the checklist at the start of each topic in this book to tick off when you have revised the notes. You should tick each section at least four times, showing that you have revised the material at least four times. These reviews will help you to understand and remember the key points, and be in a position to apply them in the exam. For each review use a different technique, e.g. mind map, revision cards, test questions, 'look, cover and test'.
- Review your notes often. Don't spend the week before the exam getting very little sleep because you are up most of the night revising. Start revising at the end of your first week of teaching!
- Use a variety of techniques to revise; even if you don't like making mind maps, the challenge of working out where material should go on a mind map will ensure you process it semantically and help your recall. It doesn't matter if the finished mind map is a bit untidy; you can always copy out a neat version to put on your wall.

A2 Specification

Unit 3 (G543) – Options in Applied Psychology

The four options are:
- forensic psychology
- health and clinical psychology
- psychology of sport and exercise
- psychology of education.

Write here the two options either you or your teacher have chosen to study.

Option 1 ....

Option 2 ....

Unit 4 (G544) – Approaches and Research Methods in Psychology

There are some new issues and debates in A2 that you need to know. These are:
- determinism and free will
- reductionism and holism
- nature–nurture
- ethnocentrism
- psychology as science
- individual and situational explanations
- the usefulness of psychological research.

The research methods section also has some new material in A2 and this is:
- the selection of a research question
- justification of the design
- matched pairs design
- procedures that generate nominal or at least ordinal data
- control of extraneous variables (participant, experimenter and situational)
- counterbalancing of conditions and allocation of participants to groups

- the levels of measurement of the data
- presentation of dispersion, data tables
- analysis of data: nonparametric tests (sign test, chi-square, Wilcoxon, Mann–Whitney, Spearman) and levels of significance (probability, type 1 and type 2 errors)
- possible future research
- alternative designs and samples.

Many of the activities can be adapted and used with other topics – try making thought clouds (page 63) for other topics, and perhaps use different colours for different topics to clearly identify the areas you have revised.

As far as anyone can enjoy having to take exams, hopefully you will find these activities enjoyable and helpful in your understanding of A2 Psychology.

Don't forget that Unit 4 is a synoptic unit and so draws on the research you have covered in your AS studies. Research evidence such as Loftus and Palmer's study on eye witness testimony could be an example of the experimental method, while Bandura's study on aggression has a contribution to make to the nature–nurture debate. The approaches and perspectives have all been covered in the AS course, and so this knowledge will be very useful in your A2 work.

For some guidance on how to stretch your knowledge of the psychology topics in A2, there are some suggestions of how you can extend your reading on page 128. This extra reading could help you write a very detailed, effective answer in your exam and, of course, you might enjoy it.

Sandra Latham

Introduction

Forensic Psychology

The specification for Unit 3 includes the following content.

Turning to crime

Upbringing

- disrupted families (e.g. Farrington et al., 2006)
- learning from others (e.g. Sutherland, 1934)
- poverty and disadvantaged neighbourhoods (e.g. the Peterborough study by Wikström & Tafel, 2000).

Cognition

- criminal thinking patterns (e.g. Yochelson & Samenow, 1976)
- moral development and crime (e.g. Kohlberg, 1963)
- social cognition (e.g. attribution of blame – Gudjohnsson & Bownes, 2002).

Biology

- brain dysfunction (e.g. Raine, 2002)
- genes and serotonin (e.g. Brunner et al., 1993)
- gender (e.g. evolutionary explanation, Daly & Wilson, 2001).

Making a case

Interviewing witnesses

- recognising and recreating faces by E-fit (e.g. Bruce, 1988)
- factors influencing accurate identification (e.g. 'weapon focus' effect, Loftus et al., 1987)
- the cognitive interview (e.g. Geiselman, 1985/6; Fisher et al., 1989).

Interviewing suspects

- detecting lies (e.g. Vrij, 2000; Mann et al., 2004)
- interrogation techniques (e.g. Inbau et al., 1986)
- false confessions (e.g. Gudjohnsson et al., 1990).

Creating a profile

- top-down typology (e.g. Hazelwood; Canter et al., 2004)
- bottom-up approaches such as circle theory or geographical profiling (e.g. Canter & Heritage, 1990)
- case study (e.g. the case of John Duffy, Canter, 1994).

Reaching a verdict

Persuading a jury

- effect of order of testimony (e.g. Pennington & Hastie, 1988)
- persuasion (e.g. use of expert witnesses, Krauss & Sales, 2001; Cutler et al., 1989)
- effect of evidence being ruled inadmissible (e.g. Broeder, 1959; Pickel, 1995).

Witness appeal

- attractiveness of the defendant (e.g. Castellow et al., 1990)
- witness confidence (e.g. Penrod & Cutler, 1995)
- effect of shields and videotape on children giving evidence (Ross et al., 1994).

Reaching a verdict

- stages and influences on decision-making (e.g. Hastie et al., 1983)
- majority influence (e.g. Asch, 1955)
- minority influence (e.g. Moscovici, 1976, 1980, 1985; Nemeth & Wachtler, 1974).

After a guilty verdict

Imprisonment

- planned behaviours once freed from jail (e.g. Gillis & Nafekh, 2005)
- depression/suicide risk in prisons (e.g. Dooley, 1990)
- the prison situation and roles (e.g. Haney & Zimbardo, 1998).

Alternatives to imprisonment

- probation (e.g. Prison Reform Trust reports, Smith Institute report, 2007; Mair & May, 1997)
- restorative justice (Smith Institute report, 2007; Sherman & Strang, 2007)
- 'looking deathworthy', (Eberhardt et al., 2006).

Treatment programmes

- cognitive skills programmes (e.g. Friendship et al., 2006; Cann, 2006)
- anger management (e.g. Ireland, 2000)
- ear acupuncture for drug rehabilitation (e.g. Wheatley, 2007).

Identify the study

Each of these boxes describes a key finding that represents a study from the area 'Turning to crime'. Identify each study and write your answer in the box. Jot down any key points you can remember about the study. The studies are covered on pages 8–23 of your textbook.

1 Brain dysfunction can be a cause of criminal behaviour.	**2** Criminal behaviour is learned from other people; a criminal does not invent it.	**3** Freudian-based therapy revealed that criminals have distorted thinking patterns.
4 Young male offenders engage in risky behaviour because they have a short life expectancy.	**5** Persistent offenders are more likely to have criminal parents.	**6** The type of offence will alter the way a criminal attributes blame for it.
7 Adolescent offenders tend to fall into three categories according to their lifestyle and personal characteristics.	**8** There may be a genetic basis for criminal behaviour.	**9** Criminals tend to be less advanced in their moral development than non-offenders.

Summary of research

Make notes on all of the studies from the topic 'Turning to crime'. Remember that there are three sub-topics and for each sub-topic there are three examples. So you should have notes on at least nine key pieces of research. You can then do the same for the other topics in forensic psychology.

Answers: 1. Raine, 2. Sutherland, 3. Yochelson and Samenow, 4. Daly and Wilson, 5. Farrington et al., 6. Gudjohnsson and Bownes, 7. Wikström, 8. Brunner et al., 9. Kohlberg

After a guilty verdict

Complete this mind map with details from the topic 'After a guilty verdict'.
If you can't complete all the details then use your notes to help you. The
research is covered on pages 54–71 of your textbook.

Unit 3: Options in Applied Psychology

8

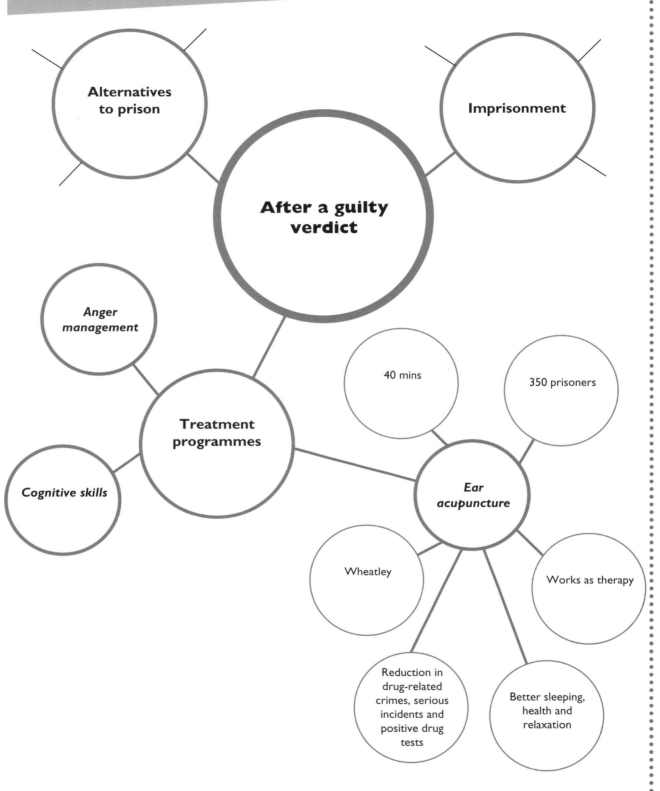

Alternatives to prison

Imprisonment

After a guilty verdict

Anger management

Treatment programmes

Cognitive skills

40 mins

350 prisoners

Ear acupuncture

Wheatley

Works as therapy

Reduction in drug-related crimes, serious incidents and positive drug tests

Better sleeping, health and relaxation

Revision card

You need to know a lot of detail about the research you have covered in forensic psychology. To help you do this you can make a revision card for each of the pieces of research evidence (theories, studies, models). It is a good idea to try and identify six key points for each piece of research. Here is a template for a revision card that you can copy onto paper and complete for each piece of research.

Name of research: **Psychologist's name:**	**Usefulness in forensic setting:**
Key features of research: 1 2 3 4 5 6	**Strengths and weaknesses of this evidence:**
Approach this research is based on:	**Evaluation issues relevant to this research:**

Perspectives and approaches

Each topic in psychology has various explanations for behaviours. These are based on perspectives and approaches. Use the activity below to explore how each approach would view the topic of forensic psychology. Which studies would support each explanation? Complete the boxes with your answers.

Cognitive approach

Explanation for behaviour

Studies to support explanation

Psychodynamic perspective

Explanation for behaviour

Studies to support explanation

Behaviourist perspective

Explanation for behaviour

Studies to support explanation

Forensic psychology

Biological approach

Explanation for behaviour

Studies to support explanation

Social perspective

Explanation for behaviour

Studies to support explanation

Unit 3: Options in Applied Psychology

Newspaper activity

Write a summary of one of the studies from forensic psychology in detail, in a reader-friendly format. Think of a headline to summarise the findings of the study and write it at the top of your article.

THE FORENSIC TIMES

The News, the Whole News and Nothing But the News

Answer the following questions using the research you have covered on forensic psychology. If you don't know the answer, use your notes or the textbook to help you, and make a note to revise that research more thoroughly. Answers can be found at the back of the book.

1 What were some of the ways identified by Sutherland in which criminal behaviour could be learned? (page 11 in the textbook)

2 What was the Heinz dilemma that Kohlberg used to test levels of morality? (page 17)

3 What did Brunner find was reduced in the family in the Netherlands who were found to be abnormally violent? (pages 21–22)

4 What did Bruce et al. find out about composite images of faces which could aid recognition by witnesses? (page 27)

5 What are the principles of a cognitive interview? (page 29)

6 What did Canter conclude about organised and disorganised crime scenes? (page 35)

7 What were the similarities between Canter's profile of John Duffy and the actual person? (page 38)

8 Which order of evidence was found to increase guilty verdicts? (page 43)

9 How did Castellow test the effect of attractiveness of defendants and victims? (page 47)

10 Who were the sample in Ross's study on children giving evidence? (page 48)

11 What are the stages of jury decision-making outlined by Hastie? (page 50)

12 What is a stooge and how was one used in Nemeth and Wachtler's study on minority influence? (page 53)

13 How did community-based employment schemes affect recidivism rates in Gillis and Nafekh's study? (page 56)

14 What suggestions for changes to prison arose out of the Stanford Prison Experiment? (page 59)

15 What were the positive effects of probation found in Mair and May's study? (pages 61–62)

16 What is restorative justice? (pages 62–63)

17 What type of cases did Sherman and Strang find were helped by restorative justice? (page 63)

18 What are cognitive skills programmes? (page 66)

19 Why does Cann suggest cognitive skills programmes were not found to work with women prisoners? (page 67)

20 How did Wheatley measure the effects of ear acupuncture on prisoners? (page 70)

Compare and contrast activity

Using your knowledge of the research in forensic psychology, think of four appropriate evaluation issues and then find two pieces of research which are similar (compare) and one which is different (contrast). An example has been done for you.

Issue	Research 1	'Compares to' – research 2	'Contrasts with' – research 3
Holism and reductionism	Gudjohnsson and Singh's Blame Attribution Inventory is holistic.	Wikström and Tafel's Peterborough study is also holistic.	Brunner et al.'s genetic explanation is reductionist.

Methodology

Each piece of empirical research can be evaluated in terms of its methodology. You might use this in the evaluation sections of the Unit 3 assessment or as evidence for the synoptic essay in Unit 4. Using your knowledge of the studies in forensic psychology, identify an example of each method and complete the chart with the strengths and weaknesses of each method.

Method	Example from forensic psychology	Strengths of method	Weaknesses of method
Lab experiment	Loftus and Palmer's weapon focus	Control of variables can increase validity by reducing extraneous variables.	Artificial situation may reduce ecological validity of setting and so reduce usefulness of research.
Field experiment			
Quasi-experiment			
Observation			
Interview			
Questionnaire			

Evaluation issues

There are several evaluation issues which could be the topic of a Unit 4 synoptic question, or could be the required evaluation issue of a Unit 3 question. Using the evaluation issues identified below, complete the chart with why each one is a strength or weakness and give an example from forensic psychology. The first one has been done for you.

Issue	Why it is a strength or weakness	Example from forensic psychology
Ethnocentrism	Research that is ethnocentric will not explain behaviour in all cultures. A way round this is to carry out cross-cultural research.	Penrod and Cutler's research into jurors takes into account only westernised courts and justice systems.
Nature–nurture		
Validity		
Determinism		

Exam**Café**

Summary sheet

This is an example of the sort of record you can make about each section, as revision preparation.

Use the Key reminder column to help you remember the name of the researcher and the nature of the research. For example, the phrase 'ear acupuncture' will help you to remember Wheatley and his study.

In the Evaluation issue column, identify an evaluation focus that is appropriate for that section. Support this with evidence or an example in the next column.

It would be a good idea to create a set of summary sheets to cover all the sections you are studying.

Forensic Psychology

Area: AFTER A GUILTY VERDICT
Section: TREATMENT PROGRAMMES

Sub-section	Evidence	Key reminder
Cognitive skills	Cann (2006)	
Anger management	Ireland (2000)	
Ear acupuncture	Wheatley (2007)	Ear acupuncture

Evaluation issue	Evidence/Example
Approaches	Cognitive/Psychodynamic/Physiological
Reductionism	Behavioural vs alternative medical

Summary tables

Check your revision skills by completing the following summary tables. The first one has been completed as an example.

Forensic Psychology – Turning to crime

SECTION	SUB-SECTION	RESEARCH EVIDENCE	POSSIBLE EVALUATION
Upbringing	Disrupted families	Farrington et al. (2006)	Disposition–situation, longitudinal research
	Learning from others	Sutherland (1934)	Nature–nurture, usefulness
	Poverty and disadvantaged neighbourhoods	Wikström & Tafel (2000)	Strengths/limitations of research
Cognition	Criminal thinking patterns	Yochelson & Samenow (1976)	Approaches
	Moral development and crime	Kohlberg (1963)	Ethnocentrism, gender
	Social cognition	Gudjohnsson & Bownes (2002)	Qualitative v quantitative
Biology	Brain dysfunction	Raine (2002)	Ethics, validity
	Genes and serotonin	Brunner et al. (1993)	Approaches, reductionism
	Gender	Daly & Wilson (2001)	Correlation, individual differences

Forensic Psychology – Making a case

SECTION	SUB-SECTION	RESEARCH EVIDENCE	POSSIBLE EVALUATION
Interviewing witnesses	Recognising and recreating faces by E-fit		
	Factors influencing identification		
	The cognitive interview		
Interviewing suspects	Detecting lies		
	Interrogation techniques		
	False confessions		
Creating a profile	Top-down topology		
	Bottom-up approaches		
	Case study		

Forensic Psychology – Reaching a verdict

SECTION	SUB-SECTION	RESEARCH EVIDENCE	POSSIBLE EVALUATION
Persuading a jury	Effect of order of testimony		
	Persuasion		
	Effect of evidence being ruled inadmissible		
Witness appeal	Attractiveness of the defendant		
	Witness confidence		
	Effect of shields and videotape on children giving evidence		
Reaching a verdict	Stages in decision-making		
	Majority influence		
	Minority influence		

Forensic Psychology – After a guilty verdict

SECTION	SUB-SECTION	RESEARCH EVIDENCE	POSSIBLE EVALUATION
Imprisonment	Planned behaviours once freed from jail		
	Depression/suicide risk in prisons		
	The prison situation and roles		
Alternatives to imprisonment	Probation		
	Restorative justice		
	'Looking deathworthy'		
Treatment programmes	Cognitive skills programmes		
	Anger management		
	Ear acupuncture for drug rehabilitation		

Look at the evaluation issues identified at the bottom of the page. All of the definitions are either unclear or inaccurate.

(i) For each one, write out an improved definition that is both clear and accurate.

(ii) Choose three evaluation issues and give examples of where they can be seen in a section (such as 'Turning to crime – Upbringing'). For example, both Farrington et al.'s study and Wikström and Tafel's study have limited samples, so you might write:

> Turning to crime – Upbringing
>
> Limited sample – Farrington's Cambridge study and Wikström and Tafel's Peterborough youth study
>
> Validity –
>
> Ethnocentrism –

(iii) Now take your responses from part (ii), and practise going beyond the superficial response. Compare like with like (e.g. reliability), ask 'so what?' (e.g. ethnocentrism) or take the unexpected view (e.g. defend an ethically dubious study). For example:

> Limited sampling in the 'Turning to crime – Upbringing' section.
>
> The Farrington et al. study into delinquent development had a reasonably sized sample of 411 subjects, making it reliable and representative. The fact that they were of a particular age (eight to nine years old) may limit its value, but as the study is longitudinal over many years, this is less damaging to the conclusions drawn. Greater limits on the conclusions drawn are placed by the androcentric nature of the research, meaning pronouncements made from this research may only apply to boys. The representativeness of the sample applies similarly to the Wikström and Tafel research in that it was a good size sample (there were nearly 2,000 subjects) and they were of a particular age (14 to 15 years old). However, this research involved males and females so didn't suffer from being androcentric.

Evaluation issues

Reliability – the study would give exactly the same results each time it was repeated.

Validity – is the study measuring what it is supposed to?

Ethnocentrism – the research is based around one specific country and cannot be generalised to the entire population.

Ecological validity – is the research based around real life?

Usefulness – is the research useful to real life?

Limited sample – the sample is small, gender-specific and unrepresentative.

Reductionism – reduced to one factor.

Individual differences – people are all different and cannot be generalised into groups.

Application – does the research link to or support the area of psychology being studied?

Subjective/objective – is the research biased/unbiased?

Ethics – is the research ethically correct? For example:
- deception – researcher has not lied to participants
- consent – consent given
- age barriers – 16+ years
- harm – no participants harmed
- withdrawal – participants can withdraw.

a) Describe research which investigates the use of ear acupuncture for drug rehabilitation. (10)

A good response

Auricular acupuncture is an alternative approach to dealing with addiction. Bier et al. (2002) trialled ear acupuncture with smokers, including a sham control group. Whereas all groups improved, the acupuncture-education group showed the greatest effect of treatment.

Examiner's comments:

Terminology and wider knowledge are shown, so this is a very good start. It is linked to the question at the start of the next paragraph.

Wheatley (2007) applied this to drug-addicted prisoners. The aim was to test the use of auricular acupuncture to treat drug addiction in prisons. Groups of 10–15 participants across six high security prisons were tested. All were on a standard care programme. An experimental group of 350 prisoners were given ear acupuncture as well as the standard care programme. They were compared with a similar group who were on the standard care programme but were not given ear acupuncture.

The procedure involved a relaxed setting, trained practitioners and the insertion of fine needles into the five acupuncture points in the ear.

Examiner's comments:

The link to the title and to crime is explicit. The details of Wheatley's procedure are accurate, succinct and coherent.

Quantitative data showed a 70% reduction in drug-related incidents when comparing six months pre-trial with six months post-trial. There was a 41% reduction in serious drug-related incidents. There was a 42% reduction in those who tested positive in compulsory drug tests.

Qualitative data falls into two main areas of benefit, namely general wellbeing and willingness to address the problem. The former includes reports of improved relaxation, better sleeping, health improvements and better communication with families. The latter includes more effort to attend classes and less hostility towards seeking and receiving help.

Wheatley concluded that the evidence supports the expanded use of auricular acupuncture and that its use was complementary to other treatments.

Examiner's comments:

The results of the research are detailed and accurate. The evidence is interpreted into groupings that are well observed and may be drawn into part (b). The final statement shows fundamental understanding.

A weaker response

A study by Wheatley wanted to test whether ear acupuncture worked.

They studied groups of 10–15 patients who were given the ear acupuncture.

Qualitative data said they felt calmer, were happier; the prison guards on the wards said the wards were calmer and there was less need to call in support services.

Quantitative data also supported the improvement witnessed, such as a 50% reduction in drug-related crime over a six-month period and a 50% reduction in positive drug testing during the same period.

The conclusion was that ear acupuncture was a good thing and should be expanded.

Examiner's comments:

The answer is generally correct but is limited and imprecise in terms of terminology, expression and detail.

b) Evaluate taking a reductionist approach to offender treatment programmes. (15)

A strong response

Many approaches have been used in an attempt to 'treat' criminals and so bring down the rate of offending.

The psychodynamic approach suggests criminal behaviour is the work of the 'over controlled' individual (Megargee, 1966). This view is not only reductionist, but is a reductionist viewpoint which is highly subjective, reducing the explanation to the innate victory of Thanatos over Eros. A treatment programme must provide cathartic activity, a little and often ideally. But again, this reduces the explanation for practice to the level of subjective interpretation of 'ego' and 'defensive mechanism', and of the assumptions of the treatment contained therein.

Examiner's comments:

This is a purposeful opening and has been referenced. The issue of reductionism is developed beyond the superficial level.

Likewise, the cognitive approach reduces explanations for criminal behaviour, this time to innate thinking, overlooking social, behavioural and biological aspects, for example. It makes the value-laden judgement of whether the thinking is irrational and maybe whether the cognitive structuring is too rigid and needs challenging. It again fails to look at the whole person, focusing on a judgement about their thinking patterns, the assessment of which is inevitably socially and culturally biased. Treatment programmes would be based on the assumptions made in Ellis's ABC of Rational Emotive Therapy, or Beck's cognitive triad, for example.

Examiner's comments:

This section of the response is appropriately detailed, shows good insight and the points are developed well.

Alternatively, the behavioural approach chooses to look at criminal behaviour as being nurtured, determined by its environment, overlooking biological and other innate mechanisms. It postulates that the social and physical environment determines behaviour, hence criminal behaviour can be modified, making it more adaptive.

More recently, cognitive-behavioural treatment provides a less reductionist account, drawing on the two perspectives, but still remains somewhat reductionist in its attempt to explain criminal behaviour and inform treatment programmes aimed at correcting that behaviour.

Examiner's comments:

These too paragraphs give breadth to the response.

Which brings us necessarily to auricular treatment. It is derived from the thinking of alternative/complementary medicine, which by its very nature is rooted in a holistic approach to cure, including criminal behaviour, treating the whole person as a complete entity. It provides a way forward, rendering reductionist accounts, which try to deal with part of the problem, inappropriate and incomplete. It possibly goes some way towards explaining why after psychoanalytic, behavioural and cognitive theories have informed the practice of so many trials and tests of so many varied offender programmes the reoffending rate in the UK remains as high as 64%. Clearly, what is now needed is a holistic approach to the treatment and rehabilitation of offenders.

Examiner's comments:

This paragraph shows good knowledge and insight relating directly to the specification.

A weaker response

Reductionism is reducing down to one thing, whereas holistic, which is the opposite, is where two or more factors are involved.

Examiner's comments:

The opening sentence demonstrates the general idea but it is not accurate.

Anger management is the most reductionist treatment because it only deals with anger. It suggests that all crime is caused by angry people, i.e. all criminals are angry, but this is clearly not the case. There could be other reasons why people commit crimes. Raine (1966) said it could be due to murderers' brains.

They compared the brains of murderers, including NGRIs (those who pleaded Not Guilty for Reasons of Insanity). They found that murderers' brains were different.

However, this is also reductionist because it says it is their brains that cause them to commit crime, in this case murder, and ignores all other factors.

Examiner's comments:

This section is generally correct, but there is a lack of detail and the concepts have been oversimplified.

> A better approach is 'cognitive skills programmes' – as can be seen there are more than one, so they are not reductionist, they are holistic. There are many different skills and many different programmes. Self-talk or CBT (cognitive behaviour treatment) to name two.
>
> Ear acupuncture is very reductionist because it just deals with one thing – giving acupuncture in the ear ... (I'm sorry, I ran out of time.)

Examiner's comments:

Comparative comment is always desirable, but this response is still very superficial and undeveloped. There are no marks and no value in suggesting that you know more but ran out of time – don't do it!

Health and Clinical Psychology

The specification for Unit 3 includes the following content.

Healthy living

Theories of health belief

- health belief model (e.g. Feshbeck; Becker, 1978)
- locus of control (e.g. Rotter, 1966)
- self-efficacy (e.g. Bandura & Adams, 1977).

Methods of health promotion

- media campaigns (e.g. Cowpe, 1989)
- legislation (e.g. Maryland study, Dannenberg et al., 1993)
- fear arousal (e.g. Janis & Feshbeck, 1953).

Features of adherence to medical regimes

- reasons for non-adherence: cognitive rational non-adherence (e.g. Bulpitt et al., 1988)
- measures of non-adherence: physiological (e.g. Lustman et al., 2000)
- improving adherence using behavioural methods (e.g. Watt et al., 2003).

Stress

Causes of stress

- work (e.g. Johansson, 1978)
- hassles and life events (e.g. Kanner et al., 1981)
- lack of control (e.g. Geer & Maisel, 1972).

Methods of measuring stress

- physiological measures (e.g. Geer & Maisel, 1972)
- self-report (e.g. Holmes & Rahe, 1967)
- combined approach (e.g. Johansson et al., 1978).

Techniques for managing stress

- cognitive (e.g. SIT, Meichenbaum, 1972)
- behavioural (e.g. biofeedback, Budzynski et al., 1970)
- social (e.g. social support, Waxler-Morrison et al., 1993).

Dysfunctional behaviour

Diagnosis of dysfunctional behaviour

- categorising disorders (e.g. *DSM* and *ICD*)
- definitions of dysfunctional behaviour (e.g. Rosenhan & Seligman, 1995)
- biases in diagnosis (e.g. gender; Ford & Widiger, 1989).

Explanations of dysfunctional behaviour

- biological (e.g. genetic; Gottesman & Shields, 1976)
- behavioural (e.g. classical conditioning; Watson & Raynor, 1920)
- cognitive (e.g. maladaptive thoughts; Beck et al., 1978).

Treatments of dysfunctional behaviour

- behavioural (e.g. desensitisation; McGrath, 1990)
- biological (e.g. SRRIs; Karp & Frank, 1995)
- cognitive (e.g. cognitive therapy; Beck et al., 1978).

Disorders

Characteristics of disorders

- an anxiety disorder (e.g. phobia)
- an affective disorder (e.g. bipolar)
- a psychotic disorder (e.g. schizophrenia).

Explanations of one disorder – (EITHER anxiety OR affective OR psychotic)

- behavioural
- biological
- cognitive.

Treatments for one disorder – (EITHER anxiety OR affective OR psychotic)

- behavioural
- biological
- cognitive.

Stress crossword

Complete the following crossword. These issues are covered on pages 94–107 of your textbook.

Clues

Across

2. What the Life Events questionnaire was actually measuring (12)
3. A combined biological and behavioural method of stress management (11)
5. A study which selects participants and tracks their behaviour (11)
7. He devised stress inoculation therapy (SIT) (11)
9. Geer and Maisel studied a lack of this as a cause of stress (7)
10. Type of networks Waxler-Morrison concluded reduced stress (6)
11. Measure of skin conductivity (3)
12. Type of events Holmes and Rahe suggested caused stress (4)

Down

1. Biological system with reduced efficiency when stressed (6, 6)
4. Things that cause stress (9)
6. Small daily irritations that cause stress (7)
8. Second component of SIT (6)
10. Where Johansson's sawmill study took place (6)

Visual organiser

Dysfunctional behaviour – diagnosing and categorising abnormal behaviour

Complete each cell with six key points from each area; use your notes to help you if you can't do this from memory. These issues are covered on pages 108–121 of your textbook.

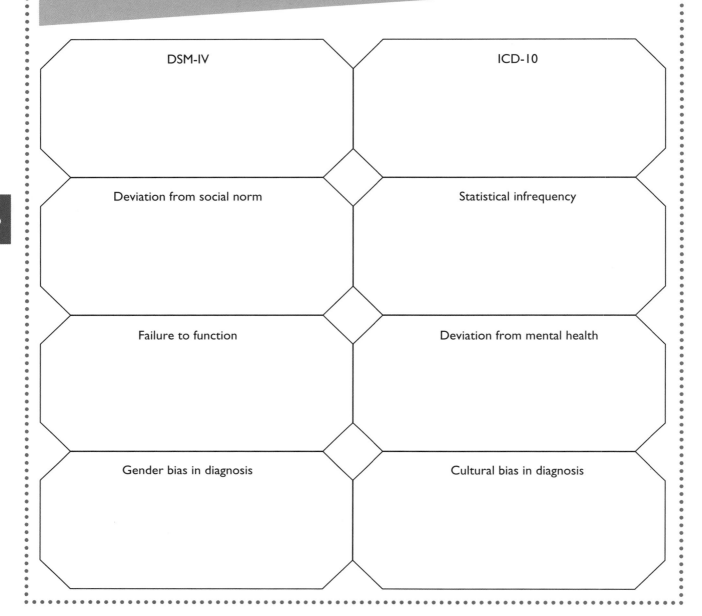

DSM-IV

ICD-10

Deviation from social norm

Statistical infrequency

Failure to function

Deviation from mental health

Gender bias in diagnosis

Cultural bias in diagnosis

Summary of research

Make notes on all of the studies from the topic 'Dysfunctional behaviour'. Remember that there are three sub-topics and for each sub-topic there are three examples. So you should have notes on at least nine key pieces of research. Then do the same for the other topics in health and clinical psychology.

Revision card

You need to know a lot of detail about the research you have covered in health and clinical psychology. To help you do this you can make a revision card for each of the pieces of research evidence (theories, studies, models). It is a good idea to try and identify six key points for each piece of research. Here is a template for a revision card, which you can copy onto paper and complete for each piece of research.

Name of research: **Psychologist's name:**	**Usefulness in health setting:**
Key features of research: 1 2 3 4 5 6	
	Strengths and weaknesses of this evidence:
Approach this research is based on:	**Evaluation issues relevant to this research:**

Perspectives and approaches

Each topic in psychology has various explanations for behaviours. These are based on perspectives and approaches. Use the activity below to explore how each approach would view the topic of health and clinical psychology. Which studies would support each explanation? Complete the boxes with your answers.

Cognitive approach

Explanation for behaviour

Studies to support explanation

Psychodynamic perspective

Explanation for behaviour

Studies to support explanation

Behaviourist perspective

Explanation for behaviour

Studies to support explanation

Health and clinical psychology

Biological approach

Explanation for behaviour

Studies to support explanation

Social perspective

Explanation for behaviour

Studies to support explanation

Newspaper activity

Write a summary of one of the studies from health and clinical psychology in detail, in a reader-friendly format. Think of a headline to summarise the findings of the study and write it at the top of your article.

THE CLINICAL TIMES

Getting Better News

20 questions

Answer the following questions using the research you have covered on health and clinical psychology. If you don't know the answer, use your notes or the textbook to help you, and make a note to revise that research more thoroughly. Answers can be found at the back of the book.

1. What are the components of the health belief model? (page 81 in the textbook)

2. What are the types of locus of control identified by Rotter? (page 83)

3. How did Cowpe measure the effectiveness of the TV advertising campaign to reduce chip-pan fires? (page 86)

4. What were the four conditions in Janis and Feshbeck's research? (page 88)

5. How did Lustman et al. measure adherence? (page 91)

6. Which psychological perspective is Watt et al.'s research on Funhalers based upon? (page 92)

7. Who were the participants in Johansson's study of stress in the workplace? (page 96)

8. What was the procedure used by Kanner et al. to assess hassles as predictors of stress? (page 97)

9. What did Geer and Maisel use to cause stress in their participants? (page 98)

10. What was the most stressful event according to Holmes and Rahe's SRRS? (page 101)

11. Outline the steps in stress inoculation therapy. (page 103)

12. What were the results of Budzynski et al.'s study on biofeedback? (page 105)

13. What type of study did Waxler-Morrison et al. use? (page 106)

14. Outline the *DSM-IV* and *ICD-10* manuals for categorising disorders. (pages 110–111)

15. What are Rosenhan and Seligman's four definitions of abnormality? (page 112)

16. How did Ford and Widiger test gender bias in diagnoses? (page 113)

17. Describe one study which illustrates the behaviourist explanation of abnormality. (page 115)

18. What are concordance rates in twin studies? (page 117)

19. Outline one cognitive therapy for dysfunctional behaviour. (page 120)

20. Compare and contrast the characteristics of anxiety, affective and psychotic disorders. (pages 123–125)

Compare and contrast activity

Using your knowledge of the research in health and clinical psychology, think of four appropriate evaluation issues and then find two pieces of research which are similar (compare) and one which is different (contrast). An example has been done for you.

Issue	Research 1	'Compares to' – research 2	'Contrasts with' – research 3
Nature–nurture	Behaviourist explanation for disorders is nurture.	Psychodynamic approach to disorders is nurture.	Biological explanation for disorders is nature.

Methodology

Each piece of empirical research can be evaluated in terms of its methodology. You can use this in the evaluation sections of the Unit 3 assessment or as evidence for the synoptic essay in Unit 4. Using your knowledge of the studies in health and clinical psychology, identify an example of each method, and complete the chart with the strengths and weaknesses of each method.

Method	Example from health or clinical psychology	Strengths of method	Weaknesses of method
Lab experiment			
Field experiment	Johansson's research on stress in sawmill workers	Natural setting leads to more realistic behaviour, thus reducing likelihood of demand characteristics.	Lack of control can increase risk of extraneous variables reducing validity of research.
Quasi-experiment			
Observation			
Interview			
Questionnaire			

Evaluation issues

There are several evaluation issues which could be the topic of a Unit 4 synoptic question, or could be the required evaluation issue of a Unit 3 question. Using the evaluation issues identified below, complete the chart with why each one is a strength or weakness and give an example from health or clinical psychology. The first one has been done for you.

Issue	Why it is a strength or weakness	Example from health or clinical psychology
Ecological validity	Research that is low in ecological validity will not necessarily reflect what human behaviour is like in real life settings; this can limit its usefulness.	Geer and Maisel's lab experiment lacked ecological validity of the setting.
Reductionism		
Validity		
Individual and situational explanations		

Exam**Café**

Summary sheet

This is an example of the sort of record you can make about each section, as revision preparation.

Use the Key reminder column to help you remember the name of the researcher and the nature of the research. For example, the acronym 'HBM' will help you to remember Becker and his study.

In the Evaluation issue column, identify an evaluation focus that is appropriate for that section. Support this with evidence or an example in the next column.

It would be a good idea to create a set of summary sheets to cover all the sections you are studying.

Health & Clinical Psychology

Area: HEALTHY LIVING
Section: THEORIES OF HEALTH BELIEF

Sub-section	Evidence	Key reminder
Health belief model	Becker (1978)	HBM
Locus of control	Rotter (1966)	
Self-efficacy	Bandura & Adams (1977)	

Evaluation issue	Evidence/Example

Summary tables

Check your revision skills by completing the following summary tables. The first one has been completed as an example.

Health and Clinical Psychology – Healthy living

SECTION	SUB-SECTION	RESEARCH EVIDENCE	POSSIBLE EVALUATION
Theories of health belief	Health belief model	Becker (1978)	Compare approaches, pros and cons
	Locus of control	Rotter (1966)	Reductionism, validity
	Self-efficacy	Bandura & Adams (1977)	Measurement, ethnocentrism
Methods of health promotion	Media campaign	Cowpe (1989)	Usefulness (application), effectiveness
	Legislation	Dannenberg et al. (1993)	(Concurrent) validity, usefulness
	Fear arousal	Janis & Feshbeck (1953)	Validity over time, generalisability
Adherence to medical regime	Reasons for non-adherence	Cognitive: Bullpitt et al. (1988)	Cognitive bias, subjective/objective
	Measures of non-adherence	Physiological: Lustman et al. (2000)	Reliability, operationalising variables
	Improving adherence using behavioural methods	Behavioural: Watt et al. (2003)	Situation–disposition, compare approaches

Health and Clinical Psychology – Stress

SECTION	SUB-SECTION	RESEARCH EVIDENCE	POSSIBLE EVALUATION
Causes of stress	Work		
	Hassles		
	Lack of control		
Measuring stress	Physiological measures		
	Self-report		
	Combined approach		
Managing stress	Cognitive		
	Behavioural		
	Social		

Health and Clinical Psychology – Dysfunctional behaviour

SECTION	SUB-SECTION	RESEARCH EVIDENCE	POSSIBLE EVALUATION	
Diagnosis of dysfunctional behaviour	Categorising disorders			
	Definitions of dysfunctional behaviour			
	Biases in diagnosis			
Explanations of dysfunctional behaviour	Behavioural			
	Biological			
	Cognitive			
Treatments of dysfunctional behaviour	Behavioural			
	Biological			
	Cognitive			

Health and Clinical Psychology – Disorders

SECTION	SUB-SECTION	RESEARCH EVIDENCE	POSSIBLE EVALUATION	
Characteristics of disorders	An anxiety disorder			
	A psychotic disorder			
	An affective disorder			
Explanations of one disorder (EITHER anxiety OR affective OR psychotic)	Behavioural			
	Biological			
	Cognitive			
Treatments for one disorder (EITHER anxiety OR affective OR psychotic)	Behavioural			
	Biological			
	Cognitive			

Look at the evaluation issues identified at the bottom of the page. All of the definitions are either unclear or inaccurate.

(i)   For each one, write out an improved definition that is both clear and accurate.

(ii)   Choose three evaluation issues and give examples of where they can be seen in a section (such as 'Stress – Measuring stress'). For example, Geer and Maisel's stress measurement may be considered an *objective* measure of stress, whereas Holmes and Rahe's SRRS may be considered more *subjective* as it is based on self-report, so you might write:

> Stress – Measuring stress
>
> Objective/subjective – Geer and Maisel's stress measurement / Holmes and Rahe's SRRS
>
> Validity –
>
> Ethnocentrism –

(iii)   Now take your responses from part (ii), and practise going beyond the superficial response. Compare like with like (e.g. reliability), ask 'so what?' (e.g. ethnocentrism) or take the unexpected view (e.g. defend an ethically dubious study). For example:

> Objectivity/subjectivity in the 'Stress – Measuring stress' section.
>
> Geer and Maisel's stress management may be considered objective as it is based on GSR measures which, being physiological, are quantitative and so less open to subjective interpretation. In contrast, Holmes and Rahe's stress measures are based on self-report, rendering them susceptible to response bias or demand characteristics, for example. It may be disputed, however, whether physiological measures are in fact immune to such influences.

Evaluation issues

Reliability – the study would give exactly the same results each time it was repeated.

Validity – is the study measuring what it is supposed to?

Ethnocentrism – the research is based around one specific country and cannot be generalised to the entire population.

Ecological validity – is the research based around real life?

Usefulness – is the research useful to real life?

Limited sample – the sample is small, gender-specific and unrepresentative.

Reductionism – reduced to one factor.

Individual differences – people are all different and cannot be generalised into groups.

Application – does the research link to or support the area of psychology being studied?

Subjective/objective – is the research biased/unbiased?

Ethics – is the research ethically correct. For example:
- deception – researcher has not lied to participants
- consent – consent given
- age barriers – 16+ years
- harm – no participants harmed
- withdrawal – participants can withdraw.

a) How could dysfunctional behaviour be defined? (10)

A strong response

For the purpose of this answer, dysfunctional behaviour will be synonymous with abnormal behaviour.

We may turn to Rosenhan & Seligman (1995), who provide four main criteria, namely, statistical infrequency, deviation from social norms, failure to function and deviation from ideal mental health.

Examiner's comments:

There is clear interpretation of terms; the introduction shows structure and knowledge.

The first says 'normal' is what the majority of people do, behaving in a way acceptable to most people. The statistical definition is based on the normal distribution curve. With a big enough population the mean, median and mode will all tend to the same point, the outlying aspects of the curve constituting 'abnormal', although commonly abnormal refers to the lower end of the curve where there is greatest need.

Deviation from social norm is more to do with cultural expectation and cultural relativism. It means there is no such thing as normal/abnormal other than as defined by society in that particular time and place. The Romans took young boys for their sexual pleasure; hearing voices was the realm of the prophets in biblical times and to the Victorians only a deviant woman would show her ankle.

Failure to function may well be less judgemental (though not necessarily so). It asks whether a person can get from one day to the next without undue or intolerable levels of distress. Failure to function is, strictly speaking, the narrower definition of 'dysfunctional' and could include behaviours such as OCD and agoraphobia. Unpredictable and irrational behaviours come under this category too. The definition is apt when distress and severe discomfort are especially applicable to the sufferers themselves as well as those around them. It is difficult, however, to be clear when acceptable levels of daily distress become dysfunctional as part of a definition of abnormality.

Finally, a notion of ideal mental health can be applied, such as that provided by Jahoda (1958). This may include being positive about oneself, being independent, being adaptable and seeking personal growth. Deviation from these would be an indication of abnormality and dysfunctional behaviour, although notions of ideal mental health are inevitably culture bound.

Examiner's comments:

The answer is well-structured, showing good knowledge and with relevant detail. The style is easy and accessible with various examples, yet terminology and knowledge are not compromised. Conceptual understanding beyond simple knowledge is shown.

A weaker response

Abnormal could be defined by what most people do. In reality, what is considered abnormal is behaving in ways that most people would find unacceptable or might laugh at. Most people have two legs so this is normal, anything else (e.g. having one leg) is not. It is not always so clear when we are talking about mental health. A very low IQ (intelligence test) indicates possible mental problems. But plenty of intelligent people have mental problems.

Abnormality could also be defined by what society says is acceptable behaviour. Lots of people take drugs and statistics show that more than half of the adults in Britain do. It would still be considered abnormal and 'wrong' to take drugs even though most people do it. Society would still disapprove.

Rosenhan said you can't tell the sane from the insane. This suggests there is no real or useful way to define 'abnormality'. However, other inmates did detect the pseudopatients so maybe abnormality can actually be defined and recognised, if only we knew how.

Examiner's comments:

This response opens with a simple, accurate statement using appropriate terminology, which could be built upon. There is elaboration by example, but the language is imprecise and there is a lack of subject terminology.

Understanding is implied but never clearly stated. The answer drifts into evaluation. As the answer progresses, it reassures the marker that knowledge and understanding do exist.

The structure is poor, and any logical progression is not apparent.

This is a poorer answer but one which would still receive some credit. Some features are better than others. Most of this answer drifts into the anecdotal despite a hopeful opening.

b) Evaluate approaches to the diagnosis of dysfunctional behaviour. (15)

A very strong response

To assess the different approaches to the diagnosis of dysfunctional behaviour we may look at classification, definition and bias. The different paradigms all conceptualise abnormality according to their own theoretical standpoints. This answer will evaluate by comparing different approaches to diagnosing abnormality and dysfunction.

Examiner's comments:

This is a knowledgeable opening that shows informed planning.

According to the medical model, mental disorder can be diagnosed by classification systems such as ICD-10 or DSM-IV(R). Whereas these systems may be accused of being ethnocentric, culture-specific systems apply throughout the world such as the Chinese Classification of Mental Diseases (CCMD). Of greater concern is the validity of classifying symptoms. Many mental disorder labels can be made up of any number of clusters within a constellation of symptoms. Schizophrenics can be withdrawn, uncommunicative and suffer avolition, living in their own worlds and in their own heads, so to speak. Equally, they may be overcommunicative, talking word salads and may show inappropriate elation. Similarly, any named symptom may be present in a number of disorders – paranoia may be part of schizophrenia, depression or personality disorder. This further calls into question the reliability of diagnosis from one clinician to the next, which may account for the fact that the agreement between diagnosticians for mental disorders is less than 50%.

Examiner's comments:

Three issues are raised here – one is 'taken further', one is well exemplified and one is well evidenced.

Similarly, behaviourists claim that symptoms define the disorder. They refute other psychological paradigms by denying underlying causes. A mental disorder is brought about by inappropriate (maladaptive) responses or a lack of appropriate (adaptive) responses to most situations. Hence, the behaviourist argues, the patient can learn adaptive responses through classical and operant conditioning, such as token economies, and will no longer be deemed to have mental (behavioural) problems. This is a reductionist view, which deals with the subjective nature of underlying causes by denying them altogether.

Examiner's comments:

There is an effective comparison of approaches in this section. The last sentence contains an effective insight.

This notion would be seen as abhorrent in the eyes of the psychoanalyst. Traumas buried in the unconscious as well as unresolved conflicts set patterns of behaviour in motion, yet are inaccessible without the skill of a psychoanalytic therapist. Notoriously unreliable, yet with intuitive validity, this approach believes that the medical and behavioural approaches are missing the key issue of identifying the underlying cause of disturbed thinking and behaviour. The psychodynamic approach only really works in retrospect and so is non-falsifiable. This is often taken as damning criticism, whereas it merely leaves the whole question of legitimacy unresolved, i.e. it means we can neither support nor refute it.

Examiner's comments:

This is another well-observed comparison; it ends with a standard criticism but this has been commented upon further than usual.

Likewise, the cognitive approach suggests it is the underlying causes, in this case the thought processes and mental structures of schemas, which account for mental disorder. Disorganised and irrational thinking underlie mental distress. However, 'disorganised' and 'irrational' are value-laden and subjective terms and Brown's view that depressives are 'sadder but wiser' supports this criticism.

Finally, the humanistic approach questions the whole notion of mental disorder, rendering the symptom versus underlying cause debate defunct, claiming as does Szasz, that the mentally ill are behaving normally given the abnormal circumstances in which they find themselves.

Examiner's comments:

This is even more breadth here, as well as good depth of analysis, which has been well expressed.

This is a very impressive answer. It has plenty of breadth, strong evidence of depth, good knowledge and expression to support extended evaluations.

A weaker response

There are many views and many approaches put forward by many psychologists when studying abnormality.

Examiner's comments:

This opening is of no value as it is far too vague.

One issue is reductionism vs holism. Behaviourists are reductionists because they say abnormality is caused by one thing ... learning.

Examiner's comments:

The candidate has the right idea here, but the statement is inaccurate.

This can be using classical conditioning where a conditioned stimulus is paired with (associated) an unconditioned stimulus that produces an unconditioned response. This association is repeated until the conditioned stimulus produces the conditioned response of its own. For example, if a dog salivates to meat then a bell is rung at the same time; soon the dog will salivate to the sound of the bell. It can also be by operant conditioning. After S-R, if there is a reward or praise for the response then it is likely to happen again. This is called REINFORCEMENT.

Examiner's comments:

This section contains description only and no evaluation, which is required by the question.

The psychodynamic approach, founded by Freud, says it (abnormality) is caused by conflict from childhood and traumas which are buried in the unconscious. Therefore, this is the nature side of the nature–nurture debate. We cannot get to these without a trained psychoanalyst. But he may interpret things (e.g. dreams) in his own way and others may interpret it (e.g. the dream) differently. This is called SUBJECTIVE. So this is not a very good approach to abnormality.

Examiner's comments:

One issue is identified and one evaluative word is used; the rest is not creditworthy. Why is this not a good approach?

The medical approach says mental illness (dysfunctional behaviour) is no different to physical illness. They still have doctors, nurses, wards, hospitals, treatment and diagnosis. This makes us think of it in the same way, but actually this might not be the best way to think of it. Whereas this approach uses classification systems such as ICD and DSM, these may lead to LABELLING. This has many problems such as treating the label not the person or giving a wrong diagnosis because the label was wrong in the first place.

There are other approaches such as humanist or cognitive, which is to do with thinking and problem solving.

All of these approaches have things in common, and all have differences. Some are reductionist (behaviourists), some are holistic. Some are subjective (psychodynamic) some are objective. Some look at the inner cause (nature), some look at the external causes (nurture).

Examiner's comments:

This section is not bad, but fails to develop any of the ideas and is rather simplistic.

They all see that ………

Examiner's comments:

There are no marks in suggesting you knew more but didn't have time to finish – the examiner will not give you marks for what you might have written.

Sport and Exercise Psychology

The specification for Unit 3 includes the following content.

Sport and the individual

Personality

- measures (e.g. Cattell's, 1946)
- theories (e.g. Eysenck, 1965)
- personality and sport performance (e.g. Kroll & Crenshaw, 1970).

Aggression

- instinct theories (e.g. Freud, catharsis, 1901)
- social theories (e.g. Berkowitz & Green (cue theory), 1966)
- managing aggression in sport (e.g. Bandura, 1961, 1963).

Motivation

- achievement motivation (e.g. McClelland et al., 1953)
- sports-specific achievement motivation (e.g. Gill & Deeter, 1988)
- techniques of motivation (e.g. intrinsic/extrinsic, Deci & Ryan, 2000).

Sport performance

Arousal

- theories of arousal (e.g. Yerkes & Dodson, 1908)
- types of arousal (e.g. Lacey, 1967)
- factors affecting arousal (e.g. Oxendine, 1980).

Anxiety

- trait/state anxiety (e.g. Martens, SCAT, 1977)
- multi-dimensional approach (e.g. Martens et al., 1990)
- models of anxiety (e.g. Fazey & Hardy, 1988).

Self-confidence

- self-efficacy (e.g. Bandura, 1977)
- sport-specific self-confidence – (e.g. Vealey, 1986)
- imagery (e.g. mental practice).

Social psychology of sport

Group cohesion

- theories (e.g. Tuckman, 1965)
- social loafing (e.g. Latane et al., 1979)
- aspects of cohesion (e.g. Carron, 1982).

Audience effects

- theories (e.g. evaluation-apprehension, Cottrell et al., 1968)
- studies (e.g. Zajonc et al., 1965, 1966, 1969)
- home advantage (e.g. Schwartz & Barsky, 1977).

Leadership and coaching

- trait and type theories (e.g. Stogdill, 1948)
- contingency theories (e.g. Chelladurai, 1978)
- coaching (e.g. Smith et al., 1977).

Exercise psychology

Exercise and pathology

- exercise and its relation to cancer (e.g. Bernstein et al., 1994)
- exercise and its relation to HIV (e.g. Lox et al., 1995)
- eating disorders among athletes (e.g. Hausenblas & Carron, 1999).

Exercise and mental health

- theories of exercise and mental health (e.g. Steinberg & Sykes, 1985)
- benefits of exercise and mental health (e.g. Leith & Taylor, 1990)
- mood states (e.g. Morgan, 1979).

Issues in exercise and sport

- burnout and withdrawal (e.g. Costill et al., 1991)
- body image in sport (e.g. Cash, 1994; Hart et al., 1989)
- drug abuse in sport (e.g. Maganaris et al., 2000).

Social psychology of sport wordsearch

Solve the clues and find the answers hidden in the grid below. This research is covered on pages 182–195 of the textbook.

```
G E K L T C C A B T E O E B I H C T
N E H O N I H O T A E G E I T O S H
I E T I D I A H H N I I V I A M O C
F O R M I N G R F E A R O C U E N O
A N E H O L P O T E S H T N T Y I C
A O R I N G E L M A N N I O E H D N K
L P A B E S A E O G N A O M R O D R
L E F T E Y I I E G L S T N E E G O
A D B O M E E R N G N N R B B T L A
I S E H C A O C N O R R A I A R L C
C E A R E T T I I L L S S L E N E H
O A N A O A N T N M K A C F G I R E
S D S I P R I T R E L E I S O E A S
E R E T U S T E T G C A O O N C O V
T E L O O T P B J I E M U I E G G S
A T J P S B A E N U N C Z T H I A E
R D S N A L M Y E R A O P S C G E N
A I H I L C K I T C B N F Y S A Y T
D R E O L F T T O L H M G T D R N E
```

1. Type of leader behaviour that is displayed
2. Final stage in group formation added by Tuckman
3. One of the sports in Schwartz and Barsky's study
4. Participants in Smith et al.'s study on effectiveness training
5. Type of audience that is doing the same task as the athlete
6. Zajonc's participants
7. Bonding of a group
8. A person's innate tendency to behave in a particular way
9. The first stage in Tuckman's developmental sequence of small groups
10. The type of advantage Schwartz and Barsky studied
11. The effect that being in a group results in less individual effort
12. What a person who does not contribute to group effort is doing
13. A characteristic which has consistently high correlations with leadership
14. A theory of leadership which suggests personality characteristics make leaders

Summary of research

Make notes on all of the studies from the topic 'Social psychology of sport'. Remember that there are three sub-topics and for each sub-topic there are three examples. So you should have notes on at least nine key pieces of research. You can then do the same for the other topics in sport and exercise psychology.

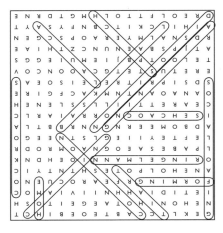

Answers: 1. actual, 2. adjourning, 3. basketball, 4. coaches, 5. co-acting, 6. cockroaches, 7. cohesion, 8. disposition, 9. forming, 10. home, 11. Ringelmann, 12. social loafing, 13. speech, 14. trait

Visual organiser

Complete each cell with six key points from each area; use your notes to help you if you can't do this from memory. You can copy and extend this diagram to include more topics in the Sports and Exercise Psychology option. The exercise psychology research is covered on pages 197–209 of your textbook.

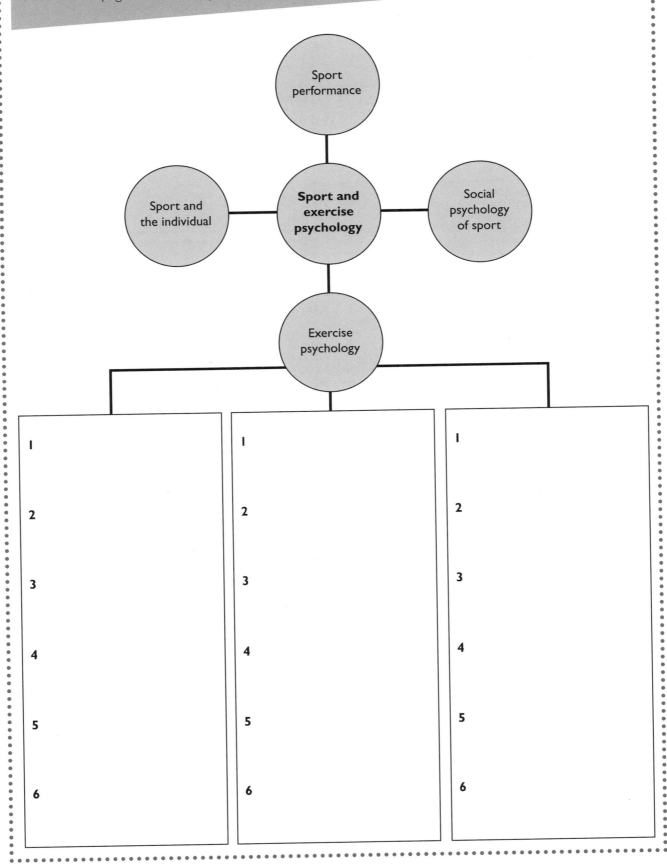

Revision card

You need to know a lot of detail about the research you have covered in sport and exercise psychology. To help you do this you can make a revision card for each of the pieces of research evidence (theories, studies, models). It is a good idea to try and identify six key points for each piece of research. Here is a template for a revision card which you can copy onto paper and complete for each piece of evidence.

Name of research:

Psychologist's name:

Key features of research:

1

2

3

4

5

6

Approach this research is based on:

Usefulness in sport setting:

Strengths and weaknesses of this evidence:

Evaluation issues relevant to this research:

Perspectives and approaches

Each topic in psychology has various explanations for behaviours. These are based on perspectives and approaches. Use the activity below to explore how each approach would view the topic of sport and exercise psychology. Which studies would support each explanation? Complete the boxes with your answers.

Cognitive approach

Explanation for behaviour

Studies to support explanation

Psychodynamic perspective

Explanation for behaviour

Studies to support explanation

Behaviourist perspective

Explanation for behaviour

Studies to support explanation

Sport and exercise psychology

Biological approach

Explanation for behaviour

Studies to support explanation

Social perspective

Explanation for behaviour

Studies to support explanation

Newspaper activity

Write a summary of one of the studies from sports and exercise psychology in detail, in a reader-friendly format. Think of a headline to summarise the findings of the study and write it at the top of your article.

THE SPORTS TIMES

Teeming With News

20 questions

Answer the following questions using the research you have covered on sport and exercise psychology. If you don't know the answer, use your notes or the textbook to help you, and make a note to revise that research more thoroughly. Answers can be found at the back of the book.

1   What are the traits in Cattell's 16PF? (page 153 in the textbook)

2   What did Kroll and Crenshaw find out about personalities and sport? (pages 156–157)

3   What is the Environmental Cue Theory of aggression? (page 159)

4   What type of motivation did McClelland et al. study? (pages 161–162)

5   Describe Gill and Deeter's research into the SOQ. (pages 163–165)

6   Who were the participants in Yerkes and Dodson's study on arousal? (page 169)

7   What are the multiple responses to arousal identified by Lacey? (page 171)

8   Describe Martens's SCAT. (page 174)

9   What is the Catastrophe Theory? (page 177)

10 What are the influences on self-efficacy? (page 179)

11 According to Tuckman, what are the stages of group formation? (pages 184–185)

12 How did Latane et al. test the Ringelmann effect? (page 186)

13 What is the Audience Effect? (page 188)

14 What are the four conditions in Zajonc et al.'s study of cockroaches and how did they affect performance? (page 189)

15 What are the conclusions Schwartz and Barsky came to about Home advantage? (page 191)

16 How did exercise affect the participants in Bernstein et al.'s study on cancer patients? (page 198)

17 What were the conditions in Lox et al.'s study on HIV and exercise? (page 199)

18 What was the sport Morgan and Johnson used to assess the accuracy of the MMPI in predicting sporting performance? (page 204)

19 What were the rather surprising results on training volume and performance in Costill et al.'s study? (page 205)

20 What was the placebo condition in Maganaris et al.'s study on steroids? (page 208)

Compare and contrast activity

Using your knowledge of the research in sport and exercise psychology, think of four appropriate evaluation issues and then find two pieces of research which are similar (compare) and one which is different (contrast). An example has been done for you.

Issue	Research 1	'Compares to' – research 2	'Contrasts with' – research 3
Dispositional and situational explanations	Trait theory of leadership is a dispositional explanation.	Self-efficacy is a dispositional factor in self-confidence.	Audience effect is a situational explanation.

Methodology

Each piece of empirical research can be evaluated in terms of its methodology. You can use this in the evaluation sections of the Unit 3 assessment or as evidence for the synoptic essay in Unit 4. Using your knowledge of the studies in sport and exercise psychology, identify an example of each method, and complete the chart with the strengths and weaknesses of each method.

Method	Example from sport psychology	Strengths of method	Weaknesses of method
Lab experiment			
Field experiment			
Quasi-experiment	Hart et al.'s research on body-image anxiety.	Allows research into conditions such as body image, which would be impossible or unethical to manipulate.	The participants' social physique anxiety scale (SPAS) score is not manipulated and is therefore naturally occurring; this can increase extraneous variables, reducing validity of research.
Observation			
Interview			
Questionnaire			

Evaluation issues

There are several evaluation issues which could be the topic of a Unit 4 synoptic question, or could be the required evaluation issue of a Unit 3 question. Using the evaluation issues identified below, complete the chart with why each one is a strength or weakness and give an example from sport and exercise psychology. The first one has been done for you.

Issue	Why it is a strength or weakness	Example from sport and exercise psychology
Reductionism	It is a weakness as it reduces complex behaviour down to too simplistic an explanation, but it does allow research to easily identify IV.	Lox et al.'s research, which attributes self-efficacy, life satisfaction, etc., to exercise.
Ethnocentrism		
Validity		
Nature–nurture		

ExamCafé

Summary sheet

This is an example of the sort of record you can make about each section, as revision preparation.

Use the Key reminder column to help you remember the name of the researcher and the nature of the research. For example, '16 personality factors' or '16PF' will help you to remember Cattell and his study.

In the Evaluation issue column, identify an evaluation focus that is appropriate for that section. Support this with evidence or an example in the next column.

It would be a good idea to create a set of summary sheets to cover all the sections you are studying.

Psychology of Sport and Exercise

Area: SPORT AND THE INDIVIDUAL
Section: PERSONALITY

Sub-section	Evidence	Key reminder
Measures	Cattell's 16 personality factors (1946)	16PF
Theories		
Relevance to sport		

Evaluation issue	Evidence/Example

Summary tables

Check your revision skills by completing the following summary tables. The first one has been completed as an example.

Psychology of Sport and Exercise – Sport and the individual

SECTION	SUB-SECTION	RESEARCH EVIDENCE	POSSIBLE EVALUATION
Personality	Measures	Cattell's 16PF (1965)	Reliability
	Theories	Eysenck (1965) (extroversion/neuroticism/psychoticism)	Validity, nature–nurture
	Relevance to sport	Kroll & Crenshaw (1970)	Usefulness
Aggression	Instinct theories	Freud (1901) (catharsis)	Disposition–situation
	Social theories	Berkowitz & Green (1966) (environmental cue theory)	Ecological validity
	Managing aggression in sport	Bandura (1961, 1963)	Usefulness (of explanation)
Motivation	Achievement motivation	McClelland et al. (1953)	Approaches
	Sports-specific achievement motivation	Gill & Deeter (1988)	Qualitative vs quantitative
	Techniques	Deci & Ryan (2000) (intrinsic/extrinsic)	Strengths/limitations of research

Psychology of Sport and Exercise – Sport performance

SECTION	SUB-SECTION	RESEARCH EVIDENCE	POSSIBLE EVALUATION
Arousal	Theories of arousal		
	Types of arousal		
	Factors affecting arousal		
Anxiety	Trait/state anxiety		
	Multi-dimensional models		
	Models of anxiety		
Self-confidence	Self-efficacy		
	Sport confidence		
	Imagery		

Summary tables

Psychology of Sport and Exercise – Social psychology of sport

SECTION	SUB-SECTION	RESEARCH EVIDENCE	POSSIBLE EVALUATION
Group cohesion	Theories		
	Social loafing		
	Aspects of cohesion		
Audience effects	Theories		
	Studies		
	Home advantage		
Leadership and coaching	Trait and type theories		
	Contingency theories		
	Coaching		

Psychology of Sport and Exercise – Exercise psychology

SECTION	SUB-SECTION	RESEARCH EVIDENCE	POSSIBLE EVALUATION
Exercise and pathology	Exercise and its relation to cancer		
	Exercise and its relation to HIV		
	Eating disorders among athletes		
Exercise and mental health	Theories of exercise and mental health		
	Benefits of exercise and mental health		
	Mood states		
Issues in exercise and sport	Burnout and withdrawal		
	Body image in sport		
	Drug abuse in sport		

Look at the evaluation issues identified at the bottom of the page. All of the definitions are either unclear or inaccurate.

(i) For each one, write out an improved definition that is both clear and accurate.

(ii) Choose three evaluation issues and give examples of where they can be seen in a section (such as 'Sport and the individual – Personality'). For example, Eysenck's EPQ may be considered *reliable* in that it is quantitative and contains a lie detector. However, Cattell's 16PF may be considered *unreliable* as Cattell himself said the outcome can be affected by mood. So you might write:

> Sport and the individual – Personality
>
> Reliability – Eysenck reliable with lie detector; Cattell less reliable as affected by mood
>
> Validity –
>
> Ethnocentrism –

(iii) Now take your responses from part (ii), and practise going beyond the superficial response. Compare like with like (e.g. reliability), ask 'so what?' (e.g. ethnocentrism) or take the unexpected view (e.g. defend an ethically dubious study). For example:

> Reliability in 'Sport and the individual – Personality' section.
>
> Eysenck's EPQ may be considered reliable, as Eysenck included a lie detector as part of the questionnaire. However, we may wish to challenge the validity of the lie detector itself, as to how effective it would actually be at detecting lies. Conversely, Cattell on the surface seems less reliable. As Cattell himself admits, his 16PF may be susceptible to mood, for example. Yet with 16 factors rather than a full questionnaire, it may in fact be less adversely affected than may be feared. This could account for the extensive use of Cattell's 16PF in sport psychology, allegedly more than any other measure of personality.

Evaluation issues

Reliability – the study would give exactly the same results each time it was repeated.

Validity – is the study measuring what it is supposed to?

Ethnocentrism – the research is based around one specific country and cannot be generalised to the entire population.

Ecological validity – is the research based around real life?

Usefulness – is the research useful to real life?

Limited sample – the sample is small, gender-specific and unrepresentative.

Reductionism – reduced to one factor.

Individual differences – people are all different and cannot be generalised into groups.

Application – does the research link to or support the area of psychology being studied?

Subjective/objective – is the research biased/unbiased?

Ethics – is the research ethically correct? For example:
- deception – researcher has not lied to participants
- consent – consent given
- age barriers – 16+ years
- harm – no participants harmed
- withdrawal – participants can withdraw.

a) Describe one technique used to increase motivation in sport. (10)

A strong response

Based in Behavioural Psychology, notably Operant Conditioning, one technique to increase motivation in sport is the use of Intrinsic and Extrinsic motivation. In Operant Conditioning, when a behaviour is reinforced, it is more likely to occur again. When it is continuously reinforced, it is increasingly likely to occur again (although partial reinforcement schedules can further increase this likelihood).

Examiner's comments:

The perspective has been identified and the word 'technique' is a direct response to the question. Clear, precise, subject terminology has been used. The explanation is accurate. It needs to be linked to sport.

Intrinsic motivation is an internal drive leading to an athlete feeling satisfied, competent and self-determining according to Deci (1975). As a drive it is never satisfied; it motivates the athlete to seek constant personal improvement and so is very persistent. A good coach therefore should always nurture intrinsic motivation.

Extrinsic motivation includes rewards such as medals and trophies, and these motivate the athlete who aspires to winning them. Seeing the winners and wanting that winning feeling themselves – this is vicarious reinforcement. When they do win, they will be positively reinforced by the great feelings of public acclaim and receiving the medal, for example. They will not win every time, and this partial reinforcement will lead to stronger motivation. The motivation to win due to avoiding the unpleasant feelings of not winning is an example of negative reinforcement. A good coach therefore needs to praise and encourage, as well as giving their charges tangible rewards if they are to increase motivation. Reinforcement as a motivator must be given immediately and in response to a particular behaviour as appropriate to the individual concerned.

Examiner's comments:

'Intrinsic motivation' is well defined and referenced. Good understanding is shown. The second paragraph introduces a practical application to sport. The structure is fluent, linking the sporting example to psychological theory. There is a direct response to the title. The explanation shows knowledge of the details of theory and approach (vicarious reinforcement, partial reinforcement). There is explicit application of psychology to the sporting context.

A child who watches Wimbledon thinks she might enjoy playing tennis, and so starts lessons. The coach should give low-level praise and encouragement (extrinsic) so as not to impede the child's natural enjoyment and enthusiasm (intrinsic). When the child does something correctly, such as tries a double-handed backhand as she has seen on

TV, the coach should give specific and immediate praise of a level that makes the child feel good (extrinsic motivation). The coach should then give backhand practice, praising the improving skill and giving the child feelings of success and mastery (intrinsic motivation).

Examiner's comments:

The final paragraph pulls it all together in a detailed and practical application and explains the technique used by a coach applying intrinsic and extrinsic motivation. This is a very good answer.

A weaker response

Motivation can be increased by using intrinsic and extrinsic motivation.

Intrinsic motivation is inside the person where they simply feel 'good' about something. Extrinsic motivation is from the outside such as money or praise.

If someone does a good job and takes pride in doing it well – that is intrinsic motivation. If they get paid quite well, they may be happy to do it again – that is extrinsic motivation.

Extrinsic motivation uses reinforcement from other people. By reinforcing the athlete they will try harder.

Examiner's comments:

This response opens with a simple, accurate statement which could be built upon. There is some elaboration in the definition of terms and a simple example. However, the use of language is imprecise and there is a lack of subject terminology. There is no explicit reference to theory. The example is imprecise, again with a lack of subject terminology. As the answer progresses, it reassures the marker of deliberate use of 'reinforcement'. The wording could be more precise.

This is used for sportsmen and women. When they win something they get medals, trophies, cups, etc. I do road running. I have done a ten-mile race a few times but I usually do OK. You always get something for finishing, even when you are nowhere near winning, usually with the name of the race on it. I have some medals, a badge, a rosette and a drinking mug. These motivate me to run another race – extrinsic motivation. Olympic athletes can win medals such as gold, silver and bronze – also extrinsic motivation.

Examiner's comments:

The final paragraph shows how the technique is **used** in **sport**, with an example. However, there is unnecessary anecdotal detail which is not framed in theory and does not use subject-specific language.

This is a poorer answer but one which would still receive some credit. Some features are better than others. Much of this answer drifts into the anecdotal despite a hopeful opening.

b) Discuss the problems of motivating the individual in sport. (15)

A strong response

There are a number of problems which can arise when motivating the individual in sport. Individual differences would suggest there is no panacea for all. The nomothetic approach of much of psychology maybe needs supplanting with a more ideographic approach. Application of psychological principles to the sporting context can be questioned in terms of its usefulness, effectiveness or appropriateness.

Examiner's comments:

This opening has a good structure and sets out the main points. It is well expressed, with good terminology and synoptic awareness (e.g. nomothetic–ideographic) which shows wider reading. A breadth of awareness of issues is indicated, as are the points within an issue (i.e. application in terms of usefulness, effectiveness or appropriateness).

One of the major problems is the issue of validity. Motivation is a social construct so is hard to define in a concrete sense, i.e. it is invisible. Atkinson et al. tried to measure it using content analysis. By responding to questions about different pictorial stimuli, patterns of language of achievement were identified. Atkinson was confident of the robustness of this identification. However, as a measure, it throws up a number of questions. Should the DV be given by the number of references to achievement / motivation or the number of different references? Should some achievement images be weighted more heavily than others? The response to these determine how the measure employed defines motivation.

Examiner's comments:

A general issue is raised. There is extended understanding and explanation of the fact that 'motivation' is hard to define, which is directly relevant to the question of validity. This is referenced to psychological research and the candidate is aware of the detail of that research (content analysis). The candidate introduces 'measure' to address validity. The positive claim from the researcher is questioned by the candidate. A specific and detailed evaluation point within the issue is considered. The impact of this is stated.

Similarly, Gill and Deeter employ a measure for motivation.

They engaged in much pre-testing of the dimension of competitiveness especially and found they consistently differentiated sports-orientated and non-sports-orientated students. This lends support to the construct validity of the measure. Further, favourable comparison to findings using other measures pointed to the concurrent validity being strong.

Being a psychometric test, the SOQ is arguably more objective then the content analysis technique of Atkinson and therefore more reliable. However, being a self-report, it allows for inaccuracy, social desirability and demand characteristics, which may reduce its reliability.

Examiner's comments:

The link sentence tenuously draws a comparison (similarity). The measure proposed by Gill and Deeter is directly and appropriately compared with Atkinson et al. and this comparison is debated, not merely presented. Higher marks are also achieved by the candidate's awareness of types of validity. The word 'arguably' shows that this candidate has more sophistication than many candidates who do not appreciate this subtlety.

In the final paragraph, the candidate develops the discussion, going beyond 'the reliability is good' or 'the reliability is bad'. They locate the debate and relate it to a broader issue, showing the synoptic element.

Note that marks would be awarded for the points within the issues identified and made, not just for the number of issues themselves. Whereas this answer does not have enough breadth to gain a perfect mark, it does show convincing insight and development of the higher order skills of analysis, evaluation and application. The mark awarded is not an average, but a judgement. If one criterion mark is out of sync, this may not bring the overall mark up or down if all other marks are consistent. The above would be considered to be a strong response.

A weaker response

> Firstly, everyone is different, we're all individuals.

Examiner's comments:

Individual differences are identified but this opening is very superficial.

> Secondly, how do you motivate someone who has lost interest? If they don't want to do something, it's not easy to get them to do it if they don't want to. Sometimes being criticised can cause negative reinforcement and cause the person not to be motivated. A friend of mine played for the school in netball, but the coach was always telling her what to do, and what she was doing wrong — in the end she stopped playing for the school (was not motivated).

Examiner's comments:

The answer quickly descends into anecdote and there is a lack of psychological knowledge. 'Negative reinforcement' is used wrongly – this example is not negative reinforcement – and the word 'cause' is erroneous. There is an attempt to support with an example but the anecdote is not linked to psychology. The paragraph shows a lack of any real understanding.

> Leonard Atkinson invented naff and nach. Nach is the need to achieve – a penalty kicker in football may want to take the kick because they think of the success. This is Nach. Naff is the need to avoid failure. Another person may not really want to take the kick because they are frightened of missing. This is Naff. Nach is better than Naff.
>
> But as stated at the start, the main problems of motivating are:
> (1) everyone is different, and (2) How do you motivate someone who doesn't want to be motivated?

Examiner's comments:

The reference should be to McClelland et al. They did not 'invent' nAff! Both 'nAff' and 'nAch' are inaccurately designated. None of these points are directly penalised in themselves but indicate an inaccurate and imprecise response. The example does, however, support the concepts and it is application, i.e. supporting evidence. Finally, although it is nice to summarise, there is nothing additionally creditworthy here.

This is a very limited response in terms of points made and richness of debate. However, it shows some psychological and evaluative awareness, draws examples and is organised, but is limited, superficial and anecdotal. This is a weaker response but with some commendable moments.

Psychology of Education

The specification for Unit 3 includes the following content.

Teaching and learning

Theories of knowledge acquisition

- stage theories (e.g. Piaget or Bruner, 1966)
- social construction theories (e.g. zone of proximal development, Vygotsky)
- behaviourist models linking stimulus and response (e.g. Watson & Raynor, 1920; Skinner, 1948).

Personal approaches to learning

- variations on learning strategies (e.g. Curry's onion model, 1983)
- differences in cognitive styles (e.g. Riding & Raynor, 1998)
- theory of multiple intelligences (Gardner, 1993).

Personal approaches to teaching

- behaviourist use of objectives and monitoring of tasks (e.g. Ausubel, 1977; Krathwohl, 2002)
- cognitive approaches of discovery learning (e.g. Bruner's spiral curriculum, 1960)
- social constructivism – cooperative learning and scaffolding (Wood et al., 1976).

Student participation

Theories of motivation

- intrinsic/extrinsic motivation (e.g. Claxton, 1992); psychodynamic theories (e.g. Freud, 1961)
- humanist 'needs' theories (e.g. Maslow's Hierarchy of Needs, 1954)
- cognitive attribution theory (e.g. Weiner, 2000).

Encouraging educational engagement

- the importance of play (e.g. Schweihart, 2000)
- the emotional nature of learning (e.g. emotional intelligence, Goleman, 1996; Petrides et al., 2004)
- the implications of ability grouping (e.g. Sukhnandan & Lee, 1998).

Student beliefs and expectations

- social roles and academic success (Riley, 1995)
- learned helplessness (e.g. Seligman, 1975)
- developing positive self-esteem (e.g. Maslow, 1954; Dweck, 2004).

The social world of teaching and learning

Personal and social development

- developmental stages (e.g. Erikson's eight-stage theory, 1963)
- the need for acceptance and approval (e.g. Rogers & Freiberg, 1994)
- moral development (e.g. Kohlberg, 1981).

Student–student social interactions

- empathy and morality (e.g. Gilligan, 1982)
- friendships/bullying and academic success (e.g. Hartup, 1989; Demetrio et al, 2000)
- anti-bullying strategies (e.g. Tatum & Herbert, 1992; Smith & Shu, 2000).

Student–teacher social interactions

- comparison of teacher/student communications (e.g. Flanders's interaction analysis, 1970)
- teacher expectations of students (e.g. Brophy & Good, 1974; Rubie-Davies et al., 2006)
- types of questions and demands used by teachers (e.g. Galton et al., 1999).

Enabling learning: dealing with diversity

Dealing with additional needs

- individual support (e.g. Bloom, 1984)
- ability grouping (e.g. Sukhnandan & Lee, 1998; Freeman, 1997)
- remedial support (e.g. Reading Recovery, Clay, 1985).

Enabling minority ethnic groups

- inter-group tasks (Aronson et al., 1978; Strand & Demie, 2005)
- role models (Klein, 1996; Demie et al., 2006)
- positive support (Mac an Ghaill, 1988; DfES, 2007).

Enabling genders

- gender differences in educational achievement (e.g. Arnot et al., 1996; Strand et al., 2006)
- biological differences in brain structure (e.g. Bee, 2000; Solms & Turnbull, 2002)
- strategies for enabling the learning of boys and girls (e.g. Younger & Warrington, 2005).

Identify the study

Match each term to the correct psychologist(s) to test your knowledge of the psychology of teaching and learning. The first one is done for you. This research is covered on pages 219–231 of your textbook.

1 Stage theory	a Ausubel
2 Zone of proximal development	b Riding and Raynor
3 Modes of representation	c Bruner
4 Behaviourism	d Watson and Raynor
5 Little Albert	e Rezler and Rezmovic
6 Operant conditioning	f Vygotsky
7 Onion theory of learning	g McCarthy
8 Learning preference inventory	h Bruner
9 4MAT	i Skinner
10 VAK	j Wood
11 Cognitive styles	k Gardner
12 Multiple intelligences	l Curry
13 Advance organisers	m Piaget
14 Discovery learning	n Rose
15 Scaffolding	o Watson

Summary of research

Make notes on all of the studies from the topic 'Teaching and learning'. Remember that there are three sub-topics and for each sub-topic there are three examples. So you should have notes on at least nine key pieces of research. Then do the same for the other topics in educational psychology.

Answers: 1. m, 2. f, 3. c/h, 4. o, 5. d, 6. i, 7. n, 8. e, 9. g, 10. n, 11. b, 12. k, 13. a, 14. c/h, 15. j

Visual organiser

Student participation

Complete the thought clouds with key points you can remember about each piece of research. Check your notes if you can't remember six key points. This research is covered on pages 232–244 of your textbook.

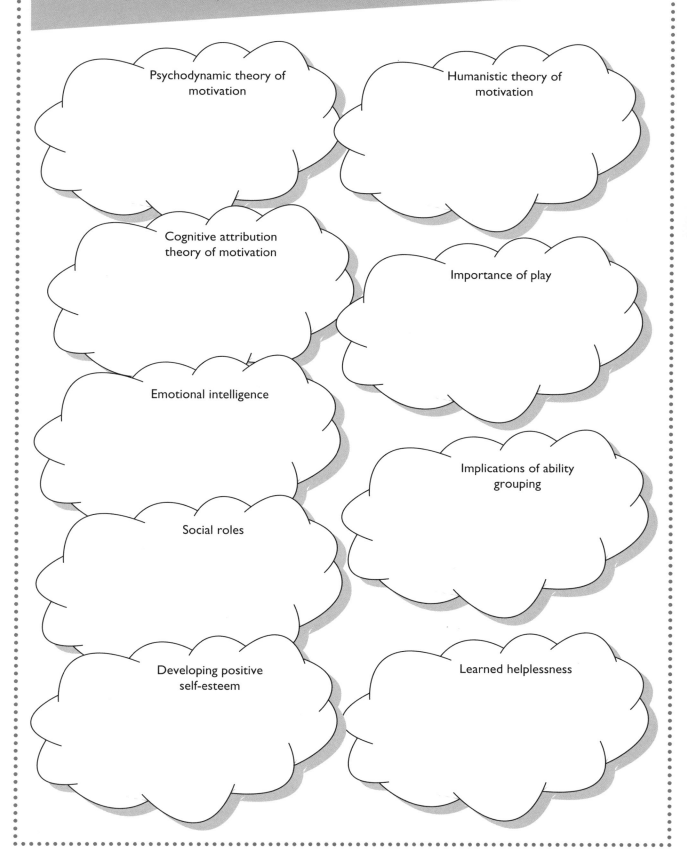

Psychodynamic theory of motivation

Humanistic theory of motivation

Cognitive attribution theory of motivation

Importance of play

Emotional intelligence

Implications of ability grouping

Social roles

Developing positive self-esteem

Learned helplessness

Revision card

You need to know a lot of detail about the research you have covered in psychology of education. To help you do this you can make a revision card for each of the pieces of research evidence (theories, studies, models). It is a good idea to try and identify six key points for each piece of research. Here is a template for a revision card that you can copy onto paper and complete for each piece of research.

Name of research:	**Usefulness in education setting:**
Psychologist's name:	
Key features of research: 1 2 3 4 5 6	**Strengths and weaknesses of this evidence:**
	Evaluation issues relevant to this research:
Approach this research is based on:	

Perspectives and approaches

Each topic in psychology has various explanations for behaviours. These are based on perspectives and approaches. Use the activity below to explore how each approach would view the topic of educational psychology. Which studies would support each explanation? Complete the boxes with your answers.

Cognitive approach

Explanation for behaviour

Studies to support explanation

Psychodynamic perspective

Explanation for behaviour

Studies to support explanation

Behaviourist perspective

Explanation for behaviour

Studies to support explanation

Educational psychology

Biological approach

Explanation for behaviour

Studies to support explanation

Social perspective

Explanation for behaviour

Studies to support explanation

Write a summary of one of the studies from educational psychology in detail, in a reader-friendly format. Think of a headline to summarise the findings of the study and write it at the top of your article.

THE EDUCATION TIMES

Lesson News, Not Lesser News

20 questions

Answer the following questions using the research you have covered on educational psychology. If you don't know the answer, use your notes or the textbook to help you, and make a note to revise that research more thoroughly. Answers can be found at the back of the book.

1   What are Piaget's stages of cognitive development? (page 220 in the textbook)

2   Describe the key features of social construction theories? (page 221)

3   How did Watson and Raynor's study relate to education? (page 222)

4   What are the dimensions of categorising learners according to Riding and Raynor? (page 226)

5   How many intelligences did Gardner identify and what are they? (page 227)

6   Outline the skills needed for learning identified in Bloom's taxonomy? (page 229)

7   What is the spiral curriculum? (page 230)

8   How does Maslow's Hierarchy of Needs explain motivation in education? (pages 236–237)

9   What effect did the High/Scope pre-school experience have on children? (page 238)

10 How were the data collected in the DfES report on pupil grouping? (page 240)

11 What is learned helplessness and how does it apply to education? (page 242)

12 What are Dweck's two concepts of ability? (page 244)

13 What did Smith and Shu conclude about anti-bullying strategies? (page 253)

14 How can the Flanders interactional analysis be used in the classroom? (page 254)

15 How did Lewis and Norwich propose that teachers could 'tweak' their teaching to accommodate most learners? (page 261)

16 Describe the Reading Recovery programme. (page 263)

17 What did Strand and Demie measure to identify the effect of language skills on educational performance? (page 265)

18 What were the key features of the Aiming High project? (page 266)

19 How do boys and girls differ in their educational performance? (pages 267–268)

20 What were some of the strategies identified by Younger and Warrington which might help raise the level of achievement in boys? (page 270)

Psychology of Education

Compare and contrast activity

Using your knowledge of the research in educational psychology, think of four appropriate evaluation issues and then find two pieces of research which are similar (compare) and one which is different (contrast). An example has been done for you.

Issue	Research 1	'Compares to' – research 2	'Contrasts with' – research 3
Determinism and free will	Learned helplessness is deterministic.	Behaviourist explanation of knowledge acquisition is deterministic.	Humanistic theory of motivation involves free will.

Methodology

Each piece of empirical research can be evaluated in terms of its methodology. You can use this in the evaluation sections of the Unit 3 assessment or as evidence for the synoptic essay in Unit 4. Using your knowledge of the studies in educational psychology, identify an example of each method, and complete the chart with the strengths and weaknesses of each method.

Method	Example from educational psychology	Strengths of method	Weaknesses of method
Lab experiment			
Field experiment			
Quasi-experiment			
Observation	Galton et al.'s study observing science teaching in Years 6 and 7.	People are seen behaving in a natural setting, providing detailed qualitative information, which can highlight areas for further research.	The observer has to infer from behaviour what the participant is intending, so interpretation may be biased or incorrect, reducing validity of research.
Interview			
Questionnaire			

Evaluation issues

There are several evaluation issues which could be the topic of a Unit 4 synoptic question, or could be the required evaluation issue of a Unit 3 question. Using the evaluation issues identified below, complete the chart with why it is a strength or weakness and give an example from educational psychology. The first one has been done for you.

Issue	Why it is a strength or weakness	Example from educational psychology
Usefulness	Research that is not useful cannot be applied in society. There are several factors which might reduce the usefulness of research, such as an unrepresentative sample.	The DfES report into pupil grouping covered only Key Stages 2 and 3.
Psychology as a science		
Individual and situational explanations		
Ethics		

ExamCafé

Summary sheet

This is an example of the sort of record you can make about each section, as revision preparation.

Use the Key reminder column to help you remember the name of the researcher and the nature of the research. For example, the word 'egocentric' could help you to remember the work of Piaget/Bruner.

In the Evaluation issue column, identify an evaluation focus that is appropriate for that section. Support this with evidence or an example in the next column.

It would be a good idea to create a set of summary sheets to cover all the sections you are studying.

Psychology of Education

Area: TEACHING AND LEARNING
Section: THEORIES OF KNOWLEDGE ACQUISITION

Sub-section	Evidence	Key reminder
Stage theories	Piaget/Bruner	Egocentric…
Social construction theories		
Behaviourist models		

Evaluation issue	Evidence/Example

Summary tables

Check your revision skills by completing the following summary tables. The first one has been completed as an example.

Psychology of Education – Teaching and learning

SECTION	SUB-SECTION	RESEARCH EVIDENCE	POSSIBLE EVALUATION
Theories of knowledge acquisition	Stage theories	Piaget; Bruner (1966)	Methodological limitations
	Social construction theories	Vygotsky	Usefulness
	Behaviourist models	Watson & Raynor (1920); Skinner (1948)	Ethics, reductionism
Personal approaches to learning	Variations on learning strategies	Curry's onion model (1983)	Approaches, validity
	Differences in cognitive styles	Riding & Raynor (1998)	Application, subjectivity
	Theory of multiple intelligences	Gardner (1993)	Ethics
Personal approaches to teaching	Behaviourist use of objectives and monitoring of tasks	Ausubel's advanced organiser (1977)	Determinism, situational
	Cognitive approaches of discovery learning	Bruner's spiral curriculum (1960)	Usefulness (application)
	Social constructivism – cooperative learning and scaffolding	Wood et al. (1976)	Situation–disposition

Psychology of Education – Student participation

SECTION	SUB-SECTION	RESEARCH EVIDENCE	POSSIBLE EVALUATION
Theories of motivation	Psychodynamic theories and intrinsic/extrinsic motivation		
	Humanist 'needs' theories		
	Cognitive attribution theory		
Encouraging educational engagement	The importance of play		
	The emotional nature of learning		
	The implications of ability grouping		
Student beliefs and expectations	Social roles and academic success		
	Learned helplessness		
	Developing positive self-esteem		

Summary tables

Psychology of Education – The social world of teaching and learning

SECTION	SUB-SECTION	RESEARCH EVIDENCE	POSSIBLE EVALUATION
Personal and social development	Developmental stages		
	The need for acceptance and approval		
	Moral development		
Student–student social interaction	Empathy and morality		
	Friendship and academic performance		
	Anti-bullying strategies		
Student–teacher social interaction	Comparison of teacher–student communications		
	Teacher expectations		
	Types of questions and demands used by teachers		

Psychology of Education – Enabling learning: dealing with diversity

SECTION	SUB-SECTION	RESEARCH EVIDENCE	POSSIBLE EVALUATION
Dealing with additional needs	Individual support		
	Provision for gifted and talented students		
	Provision of remedial support		
Enabling ethnic minority groups	Engagement and achievement of ethnic groups		
	Culture and grouping		
	Role models and positive support		
Enabling genders	Gender differences in educational achievement		
	Differences in brain structure		
	Strategies for enabling the learning of boys and girls		

Look at the evaluation issues identified at the bottom of the page. All of the definitions are either unclear or inaccurate.

(i)   **For each one, write out an improved definition that is both clear and accurate.**

(ii)   **Choose three evaluation issues and give examples of where they can be seen in a section (such as 'Psychology of education – Teaching and learning'). For example, both Bruner's spiral curriculum and Piaget's stage theory can be considered *useful* in that they have both been directly *applied*, so you might write:**

> Psychology of education - Teaching and learning
>
> Usefulness (application) - Bruner's spiral curriculum/Piaget's stage theory
>
> Validity -
>
> Ethnocentrism -

(iii) **Now take your responses from part (ii), and practise going beyond the superficial response. Compare like with like (e.g. application), ask 'so what?' (e.g. ethnocentrism) or take the unexpected view (e.g. defend an ethically dubious study). For example:**

> Usefulness (application) in the 'Psychology of education - Teaching and learning' section.
>
> Bruner's notion of a spiral curriculum has applications for the lower school curriculum, where we see that the same concepts are returned to in consecutive years, consolidating and building upon the learning of the previous year. Similarly, Piaget's stage theory has a direct impact on curriculum content in the lower school years, particularly in maths and science, for example, where the ability to conserve can be practised, developed and built upon.

Evaluation issues

Reliability – the study would give exactly the same results each time it was repeated.

Validity – is the study measuring what it is supposed to?

Ethnocentrism – the research is based around one specific country and cannot be generalised to the entire population.

Ecological validity – is the research based around real life?

Usefulness – is the research useful to real life?

Limited sample – the sample is small, gender-specific and unrepresentative.

Reductionism – reduced to one factor.

Individual differences – people are all different and cannot be generalised into groups.

Application – does the research link to or support the area of psychology being studied?

Subjective/objective – is the research biased/unbiased?

Ethics – is the research ethically correct? For example:
*   deception – researcher has not lied to participants
*   consent – consent given
*   age barriers – 16+ years
*   harm – no participants harmed
*   withdrawal – participants can withdraw.

a) Outline humanistic applications to personal and social development during the process of teaching and learning. (10)

A strong response

The phenomenological approach, borne out of the Humanistic approach to psychology, is developed from the motivational principles contained in Maslow's hierarchy of needs. We are all driven by an innate need for personal growth, whereby we strive to bring our self-image to meet our ideal self and hence fulfil our potential. This drive to achieve is the natural way of being but is, inevitably, blocked and thwarted by the social world. In children, this may take the form of waiting while other children's needs are met, or someone not liking a child or not responding appropriately to the child's needs. Learning to assimilate and deal with this is part of the child's personal and social development, and one context for this is the classroom, the teaching and learning environment.

Examiner's comments:

This opening shows good knowledge, use of terminology and the wider theoretical context. It links well to the context of the question.

The ideas of how to achieve this innate drive to personal growth while protecting and developing a child's self-esteem come from the work of Carl Rogers. The basic premise is of unconditional positive regard. This suggests that all current behaviour needs to be deemed acceptable. It should be regarded positively so that the person does not have to fight for approval or acceptance. Whatever they present should be deemed acceptable. This will give them the confidence to behave with freedom and explore behaviours and solutions which they find preferential. These should be accepted with warmth, empathy and genuineness (Rogers & Freiberg, 1994). These are qualities which the teacher needs to display to achieve the aforementioned unconditional positive regard. Where Rogers's principles derive from his notions of client-centred therapy, the same applies to pupils in an educational setting in terms of student/pupil-centred learning.

Examiner's comments:

Specific knowledge is shown here and it is both detailed and applied. Precise terminology is presented in a way that demonstrates understanding and theory has been accurately applied.

A weaker response

Maslow invented his hierarchy of needs. He put basic needs at the bottom, such as food and sex. He then had protection such as a roof over your head. Next comes belonging needs - children often want to be part of a gang, or accepted by their friends. They also want to be in a house and try to beat the other houses. It is important for them to feel part of their house. Or they might represent the school in football or netball, for example. Next up in the hierarchy of needs is esteem, where they want to be looked up to. This might be where they become a prefect, or are looked up to by others in the school in another way. Cognitive needs deal with their actual learning. Finally there is self-actualising, where their self-concept matches their ideal self. This is rarely achieved, but Einstein is an example of someone who has achieved it.

Examiner's comments:

This answer is appropriate in that it is from the humanistic perspective, but the process is not referred to. It starts and ends without application to the context of the question, but the middle examples address this.

So it can be seen that Humanistic applications can help personal and social development during the process of teaching and learning.

Examiner's comments:

This is a pointless sentence as it adds nothing to the answer.

This would constitute a weaker response with some creditworthy features.

b) Critically consider the humanistic approach to personal and social development during the teaching and learning process. (15)

A strong response

There is much to commend in the Humanistic approach in terms of a child's personal and social development. There is no moral imposition and no moralising judgement made on a child's experience. There is no pursuance of 'desirable' behaviour imposed from a higher authority who determines what that desirable behaviour is, to which we should all adhere. Such a model would be borne out of behaviourism, as expressed in Walden II (Skinner, 1948). Rather, the individual's true and own experience is central. Nor is there a therapist judging whether a child's behaviours are rational or not, as in the cognitive approach. Nor do we impose a regime of drug-controlled behaviour, to manage people to behave as we would deem acceptable. All of those approaches mean that the values of the powerful are seen as the values to be taught, but these are not necessarily the ideal values, as Hitler's Nazi Germany exemplifies.

The Humanistic approach to personal and social development can be claimed to be the most moral. Development, and the responsibility for it, reside in the learner. Whereas other approaches pursue teaching and teaching methods, the Humanistic approach focuses on learning and the learner.

Examiner's comments:

A clear critical standpoint is identified, interpreted and commented upon, in comparison to other perspectives. Detailed analysis and supporting evidence are presented. A second point is succinctly made, again with a fundamental principle well applied.

The Humanistic approach has intuitive value. The underlying drive is to personal growth, blocked by life's events and circumstances. This contrasts favourably with the Freudian approach which overlooks personal growth in favour of a sexual drive (libido). It makes intuitive sense that alongside our physical growth is mental and emotional growth too. The teacher's job is to facilitate this and remove blocks to this, allowing the natural growth to occur.

This Humanistc principle can be extended to see the teacher's role as promoting self-confidence and self-esteem. These notions of self-worth allow educational progress, in terms of personal and social as well as academic development, and the strength to overcome any adversity which stands in the way of this natural growth.

Examiner's comments:

Another point is well made here. There is good comparison, good use of terminology and good applied understanding. The answer is very clear and a more sophisticated analysis is developed.

A number of criticisms may be levelled at the Humanistic approach. It is culturally biased in many ways. It assumes that the student is eloquent and 'in touch' with their feelings. It favours those from sections of society and families who talk about their feelings and how to overcome them. As it doesn't directly address a problem, but leaves it in the hands of the individual student - problems can become stuck, or become self-perpetuating. Arguably a cognitive approach, which identifies irrational thinking and a way to address and overcome it, would be far more productive.

Finally, the features of Humanistic Psychology are difficult to substantiate or measure. Terms such as warmth, genuineness and empathy are subjective and hard, if not impossible, to measure and so challenge the validity of any proposal suggested by the Humanistic approach.

Examiner's comments:

This section contains well-expressed criticisms which show conceptual awareness. There is higher-level analysis, such as in the form of comparison.

A weaker response

The Humanistic approach could be said to be reductionist as it only boils down to one aspect - Maslow's hierarchy of needs. Behaviourism suggests at least three possibilities - classical conditioning, operant conditioning and even social learning theory. Classical conditioning says that personal and social development becomes associated with teaching and learning and so every time teaching starts, personal and social development occurs by association. Operant conditioning says that reward and reinforcement make a behaviour more likely to occur again. So personal and social development is more likely to occur if the teacher is a good teacher and praises and rewards their students. Social learning theory says that students will be aware of others' development and they might see this get rewarded (vicarious reinforcement) or imitate it and get rewarded themselves. Because of these three suggestions, behaviourism cannot be described as reductionist.

Examiner's comments:

This is an inaccurate interpretation of what 'reductionism' means. Most of the paragraph is merely descriptive.

> Secondly, the Humanistic approach could be said to be ethnocentric. In Western culture, which approves of talk therapy and recognises the pursuit of personal growth (individual), then Humanistic makes sense. But in a collectivist culture such as tribes in central Africa or a kibbutz, progress is seen as working for the good of the community or society (communism) without thinking about your own needs. So Maslow's hierarchy of needs can help in a Western society but does not explain personal and social development in a non-Western culture. Also, teaching to much larger classes, and learning by rote, which are found in many non-Western cultures, is based on Atkinson and Shiffrin's memory model, which says rehearsal leads to remembering things in the long term, whereas Humanistic and the hierarchy of needs can't really explain this.

Examiner's comments:

A second issue is reasonably well addressed, with examples, but again is rather limited. Development of the argument didn't really happen, but at least the candidate tried!

> So overall, Maslow's hierarchy of needs is quite a good model of personal and social development, but is reductionist and only works in Western (individual) cultures.

Examiner's comments:

This is correct, but is bland and overstated.

Research Methods: the Design of a Practical Project

Research methods and their strengths and weaknesses

You should know the research methods and their strengths and weaknesses. You also need to know aspects of design and procedure. Complete the chart below to help with your revision. See pages 279–290 in the textbook for answers.

Key concept	Definition	Example
Methods and their strengths and weaknesses		
Experimental	Controlled study in which the researcher manipulates variables	Lab study of the difference in memory for organised and disorganised word lists
Strength	High degree of control over variables	
Weakness		May not reflect the memory for objects in everyday experience
Questionnaire	Collection of data by means of a set of structured questions	
Strength		Large number of participants responded to the questionnaire on their attitude to smoking
Weakness	Lack of validity of responses, particularly for closed questions	
Correlation	A measurement in which the researcher wishes to find the relationship between two variables	
Strength		Can easily use statistical data from maths scores and number of hours of homework set to look for initial relationship
Weakness	Cannot infer a causal relationship between the co-variables	

Experimental designs and their strengths and weaknesses		
Independent samples		Poppy, Hannah and Alex learn the organised list, whereas Katy, Abi and Rhiannon learn the disorganised list
Strength	The same material can be used in both conditions	
Weakness	No control over extraneous participant variables	
Repeated measures		Poppy, Hannah, Charlotte and Katy learn a disorganised list followed by a different list that is organised
Strength	No extraneous participant variables	
Weakness	Order effects of practice or fatigue	
Counterbalancing to overcome order effects		Poppy and Hannah learn the disorganised list first. Charlotte and Katy learn the organised list first.
Hypotheses		
Research hypothesis		Participants will remember more words from a list of 20 words when the list has the words organised under headings than when the words are in a muddled order
Null hypothesis		There will be no difference in the number of words remembered from an organised list of 20 words than from a disorganised list.
One-tailed hypothesis	A hypothesis predicting the direction of the effect	
Two-tailed hypothesis	No prediction of the direction of the effect	
Levels of measurement		
Nominal	Frequency data	
Ordinal		Ranking in order of degree of extroversion
Interval	A precise measurement but with no absolute zero	
Ratio		Time spent reading a word list
Levels of significance		
Probability		$p = 0.05$ means that there is a 1 in 20 chance that the null hypothesis is correct
Type 1 error	Accepting the hypothesis despite the possibility of this being due to chance	
Type 2 error	Retaining the null hypothesis when the research hypothesis may be correct	

What statistical test should I choose?

Look at the different scenarios below and decide which statistical test is most appropriate for each.

1 A researcher is using an experimental method to find out if memory is different when remembering words on organised and disorganised word lists. She counted the number of correct words remembered. The same participants took part in both conditions. What statistical test should she use?

2 You have been asked to count the number of extroverts and the number of introverts in your sample of healthy eaters. What statistical test would you use to see if there is a significant difference between the groups?

3 You are required to find a correlation between the score on a life events scale and a measure of health using the number of days absence from work in a year. What statistical test would you use?

4 You have selected two different groups of students to take part in a study of their susceptibility to a visual illusion. One group is male and the other female. The susceptibility is measured on a scale of 1–10. What statistical test would you use to analyse the data?

Research Methods: the Design of a Practical Project

What level of data have you used?

Different levels of data are collected from research. Choose from nominal, ordinal, interval or ratio for the following data.

1 Number of words recalled from a word list.

2 Time in seconds taken to complete a wordsearch.

3 Ranking of female compared with male students in degree of extroversion.

4 Number of female animal lovers compared with male animal lovers.

5 Score on a memory test in terms of correct answers between old and young participants.

6 Number of aggressive acts counted from wives compared with girlfriends.

7 Preference for housework or business.

8 Number of helpers for an old woman and a young woman.

Test your knowledge

Answer the multiple choice questions below by ticking the correct answer(s) to test your knowledge of research methods. You will find the answers at the bottom of the page.

1 What is the name given to the hypothesis that predicts the direction of change?

a) ☐ two-tailed hypothesis
b) ☐ one-tailed hypothesis
c) ☐ null hypothesis
d) ☐ correlational hypothesis

2 A researcher wishes to operationalise the dependent variable. Which of the following measures is operationalised?

a) ☐ stress level of participant
b) ☐ number of daily hassles experienced in one day
c) ☐ amount of daily hassles
d) ☐ frequency of daily hassles

3 As the number of hours of television watched increases, the scores for homework decrease. This is an example of:

a) ☐ positive correlation
b) ☐ no correlation
c) ☐ negative correlation
d) ☐ positive association

4 There will be no difference between scores in a memory test between 16- to 25-year-olds and 56- to 65-year-olds. This is an example of:

a) ☐ an alternate hypothesis
b) ☐ a null hypothesis
c) ☐ a one-tailed hypothesis
d) ☐ a correlational hypothesis

5 A positive correlation can be described as:

a) ☐ the relationship between two variables where one increases as the other increases
b) ☐ the relationship between two variables where one increases as the other decreases
c) ☐ no relationship between two variables
d) ☐ a strong relationship between two variables

6 Which of the following could be described as a two-tailed hypothesis?

a) ☐ More pictures will be remembered than words.
b) ☐ Participants will remember more items when they are presented as pictures than when they are presented as words.
c) ☐ More items will be remembered when they are shown as pictures than when they are shown as words.
d) ☐ There will be a difference between the number of items remembered when they are shown as pictures rather than as words.

7 Which of the following alternatives best describes an operationalised hypothesis on gender and aggression?

a) ☐ There will be a significant difference between the number of aggressive acts committed by boys and girls.
b) ☐ Boys are more aggressive than girls.
c) ☐ Ten-year-old boys will give more shoves in one hour in the playground than ten-year-old girls.
d) ☐ Little boys behave more aggressively in the playground than little girls.

Research Methods: the Design of a Practical Project

Answers: 1. b, 2. b, 3. c, 4. b, 5. a, 6. d, 7. c

Test your knowledge

Answer the multiple choice questions below by ticking the correct answer(s) to test your knowledge of ethical issues. You will find the answers at the bottom of the page.

1 *In order to study sleep deprivation without causing harm to the participants, which of the following do you do?*

a) ☐ wake them at 5.00 a.m.
b) ☐ keep them up until midnight
c) ☐ ask participants to keep a sleep diary
d) ☐ wake participants after six hours' sleep

2 *You want to ensure that the responses to your questionnaire on age and memory remain confidential. Which of the following do you do?*

a) ☐ ask for name and date of birth
b) ☐ ask for age but no name
c) ☐ only record memory test scores
d) ☐ ask for a nickname

3 *You have used deception in your memory study as you do not want your participants to know they are being tested. You could deal with this by:*

a) ☐ presumptive consent
b) ☐ protection from harm
c) ☐ privacy
d) ☐ right to withdraw

4 *What is meant by the ethical guideline of protection from harm?*

a) ☐ protection from physical harm
b) ☐ protection from emotional harm
c) ☐ protection from physical and emotional harm
d) ☐ privacy

5 *How can you ensure that the consent you have obtained for your questionnaire is fully informed?*

a) ☐ give them an example of one of the questions
b) ☐ reassure them that they will not come to any harm
c) ☐ fully debrief them
d) ☐ make sure they understand what the study is about

6 *Which of the following is not an ethical issue?*

a) ☐ deception
b) ☐ debriefing
c) ☐ ecological validity
d) ☐ consent

7 *You have told your participants that they are taking part in a study on memory when in fact it is about conformity. Which ethical guideline have you broken?*

a) ☐ debriefing
b) ☐ right to withdraw
c) ☐ consent
d) ☐ deception

8 *Studies in psychology refer to participants by number rather than name. This is because of:*

a) ☐ protection
b) ☐ privacy
c) ☐ confidentiality
d) ☐ right to withdraw

Answers: 1. c, 2. b, 3. a, 4. c, 5. d, 6. c, 7. d, 8. c

Control of extraneous variables

In each of the following situations explain how you could control an extraneous variable. The type of variable – situational, participant or experimenter – is given for each situation.

A questionnaire to investigate attitudes to healthy eating	Participant variable
A lab experiment to study memory of faces between old and young participants	Situational variable
A field experiment to show helping behaviour towards an animal charity or children's charity	Experimenter variable
A lab experiment to show maths scores during loud music or silence	Situational variable
A questionnaire about knife crime	Experimenter variable
A correlational study of health score and daily hassles score	Participant variable
A lab experiment using a repeated measures design for memory of words in a disorganised and organised list	Situational variable
A quasi-experiment to find the difference in maths skills between two classes using a different maths textbook	Experimenter variable
A lab experiment using students and their ability to solve anagrams	Participant variable

Research methods crossword

Complete the following crossword to help revise your knowlege of research methods.

Clues

Across

1. An important ethical guideline
5. Used for repeated measures design
6. A practical application of research makes it __
9. Gives the spread of scores
10. Effect from repeated measures design
11. One measure of central tendency
13. Used in a graph or chart
15. A participant variable
16. Guidelines for conducting research
18. Consistent measure

Down

2. A representative sample
3. Error when the hypothesis is incorrectly accepted
4. Type of variable caused by the environment
7. Giving the participant an understanding of what they have taken part in
8. How likely it is that an event will occur
12. A hypothesis that will not show a difference
14. A statistical test for nominal level data
17. It measures what it claims to

Choice of materials

Do the activities below to help develop your skills in writing research materials and questions.

Questionnaire

Write a questionnaire of five items to find out if there is any difference between the clothing styles of people with different musical preferences. Use both open and closed questions.

1.
2.
3.
4.
5.

Lab experiment

Describe two word lists you could use for the difference in memory between organised and disorganised words. Hint: use animals, cars, countries and clothes as the headings for the organised list.

Organised   **Disorganised**

Animals

1.
2.
3.
4.
5.

Cars

1.
2.
3.
4.
5.

Countries

1.
2.
3.
4.
5.

Clothes

1.
2.
3.
4.
5.

Correlation

You wish to investigate the correlation between extroversion measured by a psychometric test and extroversion measured by a behavioural scale. The extroversion scale should be questions about personality and the behavioural scale should be questions about behaviour, such as 'how many parties have you been to this month?'

Extroversion scale

1.
2.
3.
4.
5.

Behavioural measures

1.
2.
3.
4.
5.

Lab experiment

You are planning to carry out a study on the effect of unsolvable anagrams on learned helplessness. Make a list of five solvable and five unsolvable anagrams.

Solvable anagrams

1.
2.
3.
4.
5.

Unsolvable anagrams

1.
2.
3.
4.
5.

Possible future research, alternative designs and samples

Read the following research projects and suggest possible future research, an alternative design and an alternative sample

Experimental method

Your research project measures the differences between 16- to 25-year-olds and 45- to 60-year-olds in their ability to remember the details from a fairy tale that is read out to them under controlled conditions.

Possible future research

Alternative design

Alternative sample

Correlation

Your research project measures the relationship between the number of police patrolling the streets and the number of crimes committed in the area. You use data from Home Office statistics.

Possible future research

Alternative design

Alternative sample

Questionnaire

You have designed a questionnaire to find out the differences between males and females in their reasons for choosing a university course in Psychology.

Possible future research

Alternative design

Alternative sample

Writing hypotheses

For the following research questions, write a testable alternate hypothesis and a null hypothesis.

Research question	Does the presence of a weapon affect the correct identification of a suspect in a line-up?
Alternate hypothesis	
Null hypothesis	

Research question	Are students who have received empathy training less likely to bully other students?
Alternate hypothesis	
Null hypothesis	

Research question	Will there be a positive correlation between daily hassles and health?
Alternate hypothesis	
Null hypothesis	

Research question	Will a drink-driving media campaign affect drinking behaviour?
Alternate hypothesis	
Null hypothesis	

Choosing your sample

For each of the following research questions, identify a target population, then choose a sampling method, describe a sample and give one strength and one weakness of this sample.

Research question	The effect of an audience on the performance of basketball
Target population	
Sampling method	
Sample	
Strength	
Weakness	

Research question	The reduction of exam stress by the use of biofeedback techniques
Target population	
Sampling method	
Sample	
Strength	
Weakness	

Research question	Gender differences in the fear of inner city knife crime
Target population	
Sampling method	
Sample	
Strength	
Weakness	

Describing your data

For the following sets of data describe how you would present this data in terms of the data table and graph to be used and the measure of central tendency and dispersion.

I Number of words remembered

Three to four letters long		Seven to eight letters long	
Emily	9	Katie	6
Jess	11	Frank	4
Dave	10	Sasha	5
Louise	8	Jenny	9
Isobel	10	Chris	5

_____

_____

_____

_____

_____

_____

_____

_____

2 Researchers want to find a relationship between the scores in a Maths test and the scores in a Physics test.

	Maths test score	Physics test score
Maisie	22	25
Ron	19	7
Sam	25	10
Charlotte	15	17
Ben	18	20

_____

_____

_____

_____

_____

_____

_____

_____

ExamCafé

Research methods: the design of a practical project

What the exam looks like

Sample methods question in Section A

Questionnaires are widely used by psychologists to find out the attitudes and values of members of the general public. One of the problems with this data is that it relies on people being honest about their beliefs. The following topics could be tested on male and female participants or young and old to see the difference in their attitudes:

- couples living together before marriage
- advertising of junk food on television
- share of domestic chores between men and women
- the role of teenagers in knife crime
- stop and search of black youths
- religious beliefs.

You are required to develop a research question based on one of the above topics.

Answer **all** the following questions in relation to one topic.

1. State a null hypothesis for your investigation. (3)

2. Describe the procedure for your investigation.
   Marks are awarded for how appropriate the procedure is for testing the hypothesis as well as how feasible it would be to replicate the investigation. (13 + 6)

3. What descriptive statistic would you use to describe your data? (3)

4. Discuss the validity of this measure. (6)

5. Describe an alternative sample you could have used in this study. (3)

6. What effect will an alternative sample have on the results of your study? Give reasons for your answer. (3)

7. Are there any ethical issues you would have considered in conducting this research? (3)

Candidate A's choice of research question

Advertising of junk food on television

Examiner's comments:

The candidate should choose a topic that they are familiar with and think about how they could apply it to the following questions before starting to answer them.

Exam question

1. State a null hypothesis for your investigation. (3)

Candidate's answer

There will be no difference in the attitude score of participants measured out of 25 from questions in a questionnaire about advertising of junk food between 3 pm and 8 pm and advertising of junk food between 8 pm and midnight. (Junk food is categorised as any food product which has a higher than 10% fat or sugar content.)

Examiner's comments:

In itself the research question does not provide a hypothesis and so the candidate must develop an appropriate idea. The suggestion of different attitudes to early and late viewing times is topical and testable. The hypothesis may seem a little wordy but an operationalised hypothesis is expected with the IV and DV clearly measurable.

Exam question

2. Describe the procedure for your investigation.

   Marks are awarded for how appropriate the procedure is for testing the hypothesis as well as how feasible it would be to replicate the investigation. (13 + 6)

Candidate's answer

The researcher developed a questionnaire in order to find out if students thought that junk food adverts should only be shown late in the evening so that children would be less likely to see them. The questions were developed by the researcher and not taken from an existing test. Here are two examples of the questions used.

Q1. On a scale of 1–10 where 1 = not appropriate and 10 = very appropriate, what number would you give to the following?
a) showing junk food adverts between 3 pm and 8 pm
b) showing junk food adverts between 8 pm and midnight

Q2. On a scale of 1–5 where 1 = strongly disagree and 5 = strongly agree, what number would you give to the following?
a) Junk food adverts shown between 3 pm and 8 pm will have a bad influence.
b) Junk food adverts shown between 8 pm and midnight will have a bad influence.

An opportunity sample of 12 psychology students from an A2 psychology lesson were invited to fill out a questionnaire in the classroom during an 11.00 am lesson. The whole class took part and sat separately and filled out the questionnaire in silence. The experimenter gave the following instructions: 'Please will you spend three minutes answering the following five questions about junk food advertising on television.' The questionnaires were taken in and the scores added up for the students' attitudes to junk food adverts shown between 3 pm and 8 pm and attitudes to junk food adverts shown between 8 pm and midnight. The students were thanked and debriefed and told the results of the study.

Examiner's comments:

This is a detailed answer, but for 19 marks a detailed description is needed and it should be in enough detail that the procedure could be replicated. Two or three questions would be enough to get an understanding of the nature of the questions used. It is important that the sample, testing conditions and the conditions being tested are all described. The sample and sampling method have been described here, but this could have been done more fully. The candidate might have described the IV and DV more clearly and explained that each participant is used in both conditions hence making the design a repeated measures design.

Exam question

3. What descriptive statistic would you use to describe your data? (3)

Candidate's answer

The quantitative data provides a numerical score for each participant out of 25 for each condition. Each participant would have a score for attitude to junk food adverts between 3 pm and 8 pm and attitude to junk food adverts between 8 pm and midnight. A mean score for participants in the two conditions would show the difference between the two conditions.

Examiner's comments:

This is a good answer to this question and relates to the context of the study.

Exam question

4. Discuss the validity of this measure. (6)

Candidate's answer

This may not be completely valid as a topic such as junk food in the media is very topical and so participants may give socially desirable answers even if they don't really think that children should not be exposed to junk food adverts.

Examiner's comments:

This is a relevant answer showing awareness of the meaning of validity. However, as this is a six-mark question, it needs to be answered with a few more examples.

Exam question

5. Describe an alternative sample you could have used in this study. (3)

Candidate's answer

Instead of using psychology students, an alternative sample could have been members of the public. The researcher could go into a town centre (for example, Reading) on a Saturday morning and use an opportunity sample of the first 20 willing people that are passing by (they should exclude under 16s or very old people aged over 80).

Examiner's comments:

This is an appropriate alternative sample but details of gender and occupational group would give more detail.

Exam question

6. What effect will an alternative sample have on the results of your study. Give reasons for your answer. (3)

Candidate's answer

This alternative sample of members of the general public is a more representative sample of views on junk food. Students are one age and relatively educated. Psychology students may be more likely to show demand characteristics than older participants who may not be so conscious of expected results.

Examiner's comments:

The student has highlighted the main differences between the two samples but has failed to directly address the difference this would make to the results. The general public may give less socially desirable answers and be less concerned about the risks to health of showing junk food adverts to children. Hence the difference between the results in the two conditions would be smaller for this alternative sample.

Exam question

7. Are there any ethical issues you would have considered in conducting this research? (3)

Candidate's answer

I would have considered the issue of confidentiality and therefore would not have had any names on the question papers so that the students would not be embarrassed to write down what they thought about junk food. I would also have considered the issue of protection and made sure that the questions were not personal and were not about how they themselves were affected by junk food. By keeping to asking about their attitudes there would be no reason for the participants to feel embarrassed about their own TV watching or their eating behaviour.

Examiner's comments:

This is a very detailed and clear explanation of relevant ethical issues discussed in the context of this study.

Candidate B's choice of research question

Share of domestic chores between men and women

Examiner's comments:

This is a good topic to choose as students may be familiar with studies on gender differences.

Exam question

1. State a null hypothesis for your investigation. (3)

Candidate's answer

There will be no difference in the number of domestic chores participants expect females and their male partners to undertake.

Examiner's comments:

The student has correctly identified a null hypothesis but it is not clear how the dependent variable will be measured. The student could have referred to their questionnaire and clarified what they meant by domestic chore.

Exam question

2. Describe the procedure for your investigation.

   Marks are awarded for how appropriate the procedure is for testing the hypothesis as well as how feasible it would be to replicate the investigation. (13 + 6)

Candidate's answer

The researcher developed a questionnaire in order to find out if participants think men and women differ in the number of domestic chores they should undertake. He made up a questionnaire to ask these questions and went into Oxford Street, London, and asked passers-by their views. He asked the first twenty people who were willing to stop to fill out the questionnaire. It only took them about one minute to do this and he thanked them for their time. He added up the scores to see if people thought there was a difference in the responsibility of men and women to do such things as washing up or taking out the rubbish.

Examiner's comments:

This is not a detailed enough response for a 19-mark question. It should include details of the sample, e.g. the approximate age and gender of the participants and of the sampling method. Even if all the questions are not included, credit will be given for details of materials used, which includes the questions and the way they were constructed. It is important for the student to give details of the conditions under which participants are tested as this can affect their response. It should be clear from this description what the IV and DV are and what design is used, i.e. in this case repeated measures, as the participants are tested in both conditions.

Exam question

3. What descriptive statistic would you use to describe your data? (3)

Candidate's answer

I would use a bar chart to describe my data.

Examiner's comments:

This is an appropriate answer but should be described more fully in terms of what data will be used in the bar chart and how the variables will be drawn. A diagram would enhance the quality of the response.

Exam question

4. Discuss the validity of this measure. (6)

Candidate's answer

It would be valid to describe data in terms of mean number of chores that should be done by males and females as this is a direct measure of their attitude to male and female roles.

Examiner's comments:

A better answer would focus on the problems of measuring attitudes in a questionnaire because of problems such as social desirability bias.

Exam question

5. Describe an alternative sample you could have used in this study. (3)

Candidate's answer

Instead of using people in Oxford Street I could use an opportunity sample of students in my college and hence get a sample of views of 16- to 19-year-olds.

Examiner's comments:

The description of a sample should always include number of participants, their age, occupation, etc.

Exam question

6. What effect will an alternative sample have on the results of your study. Give reasons for your answer. (3)

Candidate's answer

This alternative sample of students at my college would be less representative of the general population as they are all a similar age and cognitive ability. Students would be more aware of the importance of equality of sharing domestic chores and so would be less likely to show a difference than the original sample.

Examiner's comments:

This is a reasonable answer, although the reason for the difference in results expected could have been more fully elaborated.

Exam question

7. Are there any ethical issues you would have considered in conducting this research? (3)

I would have considered the issue of consent and made sure that the participants knew what the study was about when agreeing to take part.

Examiner's comments:

This answer is correct but could have been put into context and another issue such as confidentiality might have been mentioned as well.

Your answers to a similar question

Now try the same questions yourself (see page 94) but using the research topic of 'the role of teenagers in knife crime'.

Approaches, Perspectives, Methods, Issues and Debates

Terms and concepts

You should know and understand all of the following terms and concepts covering approaches, perspectives, methods, issues and debates. Fill in the gaps to check your knowledge.

Key concept	Definition	Example
Approaches		
Physiological		The role of the neurotransmitter serotonin in depression
Cognitive	This approach emphasises the importance of mental processes	Thinking, memory and language are cognitive processes
Individual differences	This approach recognises that the human condition is extremely diverse	
Developmental		Piaget demonstrates that children's thinking progresses through a series of stages
Social	This approach is concerned with how the individual relates to others	Social identity theory emphasises the role of the group in forming our identity
Perspectives		
Behaviourist	This perspective limits the study of psychology to observable behaviour only.	
Psychodynamic		The subconscious is revealed in dreams and fantasies
Methods		
Experimental (laboratory)		Castellow's experiment on the effects of attractiveness on jury verdicts
Experimental (field)	An experiment which is carried out in the natural environment	Piliavin's subway Samaritan study is carried out on the NY subway
Case study		Freud's study of Little Hans and his phobia
Self-report	The data gathered from interviews, questionnaires and psychometric tests	
Observation		Observation of coaches in Smith's study of coach effectiveness training

Key concept	Definition	Example
Methodological issues		
Reliability		
Validity		
Issues		
Ethics		
Ecological validity		High ecological validity in Ost and Westling's treatment of panic attacks
Longitudinal and snapshot		Snapshot study, e.g. Strand et al.'s study measuring cognitive ability in a 'one off' test
Qualitative and quantitative data		
Debates		
Determinism and free will		
Reductionism and holism		
Nature–nurture	Nature – behaviour is determined by hereditary factors, whereas nurture suggests that behaviour is shaped by the environment	Nurture – from the Education section, Younger and Warrington highlight that all children can benefit from good teaching Nature – from the Sport section, Kroll and Crenshaw investigated the link between personality and choice of sport
Ethnocentrism		
Psychology as science	A discussion as to whether psychology has scientific features such as objectivity	
Individual and situational explanations		
The usefulness of psychological research		

Research examples

Use the grid on this page and on page 105 to support your revision for Options 1 and 2 – Forensic, Sport and Exercise, Health and Clinical, or Education. (Make a copy of the pages for each option.) Select one piece of research to support each approach, perspective, method, issue or debate listed. Identify a strength and weakness of each piece of research.

	Research example	Strength	Weakness
Approach			
Physiological			
Cognitive			
Individual differences			
Developmental			
Social			
Perspective			
Behaviourist			
Psychodynamic			
Method			
Experimental (lab)			
Experimental (field)			
Case study			
Self-report			
Observation			

	Research example	Strength	Weakness
Issue			
Ethics			
Ecological validity			
Longitudinal and snapshot			
Qualitative and quantitative			
Debate			
Determinism			
Reductionism			
Nature–nurture			
Ethnocentrism			
Psychology as science			
Individual and situational explanations			
Usefulness			
	Research example	Strength	Weakness

Research methods and issues

The following pieces of research are described in the A2 textbook. Can you choose the method that is used to carry them out and select an issue (ethics, ecological validity, longitudinal and snapshot, qualitative and quantitative data) that might be highlighted?

Research	Method	Issue with context
FORENSICS – the Peterborough Youth Study	Self-report	Qualitative and quantitative data collected on e.g. percentage of males who committed a crime and nature of crimes
FORENSICS – Bruce, 1988 – recognising faces		
FORENSICS – Loftus et al. – weapon focus		
FORENSICS – Fisher et al. – test of the cognitive interview		
FORENSICS – Canter – the case of John Duffy	Case study	
FORENSICS – Asch – the power of majority influence and conformity		Ethics – deception, as participants did not know that the other people were stooges of the experimenter
FORENSICS – study of John following a cognitive behaviour programme called CALM		
FORENSICS – Sherman and Strang – review of restorative justice		
HEALTH – Janis and Feshbeck – effects of fear arousal	Experiment	
HEALTH – Watt et al. – improving adherence to taking asthma medication using a Funhaler		
HEALTH – Johansson et al. – measurement of stress response		
HEALTH – Kanner et al. – hassles and uplifts scale	Self-report	
HEALTH – Holmes and Rahe – life events as stressors		Validity, as different events mean different things to different people
HEALTH – Ford and Widiger – sex bias in the diagnosis of disorders		
HEALTH – McGrath – successful treatment of a noise phobia		
HEALTH – Ohman et al. – types of phobia and biological predisposition to them		Ethics of inducing phobias in people despite their consent

Research methods and issues

The following pieces of research are described in the A2 textbook. Can you choose the method that is used to carry them out and select an issue (ethics, ecological validity, longitudinal and snapshot, qualitative and quantitative data) that might be highlighted?

Research	Method	Issue with context
SPORT – Cattell's 16PF		
SPORT – Gill and Deeter – sports orientation questionnaire	Self-report	
SPORT – Yerkes and Dodson – the 'dancing mice' study		
SPORT – Martens – competitive state anxiety inventory		Quantitative data from questionnaire
SPORT – Cottrell et al. – the effects of an audience		
SPORT – Zajonc et al. – cockroach studies	Experiment	
SPORT – Smith et al. – coach effectiveness training		
SPORT – Maganaris et al. – psychological expectancy effects using a steroid placebo		Longitudinal study of power lifters over a number of trials
EDUCATION – Wood et al. – the role of tutoring in problem solving	Observation	
EDUCATION – Schweihart – the High/Scope pre-school study		Longitudinal study of pre-school provision
EDUCATION – Petrides et al. – the role of trait emotional intelligence		
EDUCATION – Hirohito and Seligman – learned helplessness	Lab experiment	
EDUCATION – Smith and Shu – what good schools can do about bullying		Longitudinal survey on the effectiveness of anti-bullying strategies
EDUCATION – Rubie-Davies et al. – expecting the best for students		
EDUCATION – Galton et al. – continuity and progression in Science teaching		

Research approaches/perspectives and debates

The following pieces of research are described in the A2 book. Can you choose the approach/perspective that they are from and select a debate (determinism, reductionism, nature–nurture, ethnocentrism, psychology as science, individual and situational explanations and usefulness) that might be discussed using this evidence?

Research	Approach	Debate with context
FORENSICS – Farrington et al. – the Cambridge study		
FORENSICS – Fisher et al. – the cognitive interview	Cognitive	
FORENSICS – Raine – understanding antisocial behaviour in children		
FORENSICS – Christiansen – twin studies	Physiological	
FORENSICS – Loftus et al. – facts about 'weapon focus'		
FORENSICS – Canter et al. – test of organised/disorganised typologies		
HEALTH – McGrath – treatment of noise phobia with systematic desensitisation		Useful to find an effective treatment for phobia
HEALTH – Leibowitz – treatment of phobia with phenelzine		
HEALTH – Ost and Westling – treatment of panic attacks with CBT	Cognitive and behaviourist	
HEALTH – Lewinsohn et al. – positive reinforcement and depression		
HEALTH – Gottesman and Shields – twin studies of schizophrenia		Determinist to focus on biological explanations for schizophrenia
HEALTH – Paul and Lentz – social learning to help psychotic patients		

Research approaches/perspectives and debates

The following pieces of research are described in the A2 book. Can you choose the approach/perspective that they are from and select a debate (determinism, reductionism, nature–nurture, ethnocentrism, psychology as science, individual and situational explanations and usefulness) that might be discussed using this evidence?

Research	Approach	Debate
SPORT – Steinberg and Sykes – the endorphin hypothesis		
SPORT – Eysenck – personality theory		
SPORT – Berkowitz and Geen – environmental cue theory		Situational explanation for aggressive behaviour rather than individual
SPORT – Freud's theory of aggression		
SPORT – Gill and Deeter – sports orientation questionnaire		Quantitative data from SOQ gives a numerical comparison of competitiveness
SPORT – Lacey – somatic response patterning		
EDUCATION – Erikson – developmental stages		Useful for teachers to know the conflicts that children are experiencing at the different stages of development
EDUCATION – Weiner – cognitive attribution theory	Cognitive	
EDUCATION – Freud – drive reduction theory		
EDUCATION – Bruner – discovery learning		
EDUCATION – Gardner – theory of multiple intelligences		The emphasis on multiple intelligences takes a holistic view of the child (rather than reductionist)
EDUCATION – Watson and Raynor – conditioned emotional response	Behaviourist	

Approaches and perspectives

Test your knowledge of approaches and perspectives in psychology by filling in the blanks.

The cognitive approach to psychology is concerned with **1**_____ mental processes, in contrast to the social approach, which is more concerned with the external influences of the **2**_____ and cultural environment. Cognitive psychologists frequently conduct research using the **3**_____ method and, because extraneous variables are strictly controlled, causal relationships can be inferred. Social psychologists may conduct their research in the laboratory, but many studies take place in the natural environment. For example, Piliavin used a **4**_____ **5**_____ to investigate helping behaviour on the New York subway.

The developmental approach to psychology is concerned with the changes that occur in a person's **6**_____. This can be the result of lifetime experiences or because of inherited factors (**7**_____ – **8**_____ debate). On the other hand the physiological approach is considered to be more **9**_____, that is, it does not take into account the broader sense of what it is to be human and limits its explanations of behaviour to **10**_____ ones. This approach suggests that people do not have the ability to choose their own course of action, that is have free will, but that their behaviour is **11**_____ by internal bodily processes. Many developmental studies are longitudinal. For example, Kohlberg studied the developmental stages of morality over a number of years. However, physiological approach studies may be **12**_____ and only look at the behaviour that is occurring at that point in time.

The psychodynamic perspective is very different from the behaviourist perspective as it emphasises the importance of the **13**_____, whereas behaviourists argue that in order to call itself a science psychology should be confined to observable **14**_____. B. F. Skinner is famous for his theory of **15**_____ conditioning developed from his work with pigeons and rats, whereas Sigmund Freud is famous for his **16**_____ theory developed from his work with neurotic female patients. However, both these men have made a considerable contribution to the treatment of various **17**_____ disorders. Lewinsohn has demonstrated that depressed patients have their mood lifted by **18**_____ events (behaviourist) and many modern therapists use techniques developed by **19**_____ and his followers.

Answers: 1. internal, 2. social, 3. experimental, 4. field, 5. experiment, 6. lifespan, 7. nature, 8. nurture, 9. reductionist, 10. biological, 11. determined, 12. snapshot, 13. unconscious, 14. behaviour, 15. operant, 16. psychoanalytic, 17. mental, 18. pleasant, 19. Freud.

Test your knowledge

Answer the multiple choice questions below by ticking the correct answer(s) to test your knowledge of approaches and perspectives. You will find the answers at the bottom of the page.

1 The original psychodynamic theory was developed by which of the following psychologists?

a) ☐ Carl Jung
b) ☐ Sigmund Freud
c) ☐ Erik Erikson
d) ☐ Hans Eysenck

2 A major criticism of the theories in the psychodynamic approach is that they are:

a) ☐ idealistic
b) ☐ precise
c) ☐ vague
d) ☐ untestable

3 A characteristic of the developmental approach is that the studies are often:

a) ☐ longitudinal
b) ☐ looking for changes
c) ☐ about children
d) ☐ all three of the above

4 The social psychology approach can help us understand how we behave when we are:

a) ☐ in the field
b) ☐ in groups
c) ☐ alone
d) ☐ in a lab

5 Behaviourists believe that our behaviour is shaped by:

a) ☐ innate factors
b) ☐ the mother
c) ☐ the environment
d) ☐ the genes

6 An assumption of the physiological approach is that behaviour is determined by:

a) ☐ biological processes
b) ☐ genetic factors
c) ☐ the nervous system
d) ☐ all of the above

7 Behaviour modification and behaviour therapy are based on the principles of which approach?

a) ☐ behaviourist approach
b) ☐ individual differences approach
c) ☐ developmental approach
d) ☐ cognitive approach

Test your knowledge

Answer the multiple choice questions below by ticking the correct answer(s) to test your knowledge of issues and debates. You will find the answers at the bottom of the page.

1   *One of the BPS ethical guidelines referring to keeping participants from harm is referred to as:*

a)   ☐ protection
b)   ☐ confidentiality
c)   ☐ right to withdraw
d)   ☐ debriefing

2   *One of the characteristics of psychology that help define it as a science is the use of:*

a)   ☐ electric shocks
b)   ☐ the case study method
c)   ☐ hypothesis testing
d)   ☐ qualitative data

3   *An attempt to explain something in terms of its component parts may be thought of as:*

a)   ☐ holistic
b)   ☐ reductionist
c)   ☐ biological
d)   ☐ determinist

4   *Psychodynamic theorists and behaviourists do not believe in free will. This means that their theories are heavily:*

a)   ☐ Freudian
b)   ☐ deterministic
c)   ☐ antisocial
d)   ☐ reductionist

5   *Many psychologists emphasise the importance of childhood experiences in shaping behaviour. In the nature–nurture debate, this supports:*

a)   ☐ nature
b)   ☐ nature–nurture
c)   ☐ nurture
d)   ☐ none of the above

6   *Most psychological research is carried out in the USA and this may account for the emphasis on the Western perspective, which is an example of:*

a)   ☐ ethnocentrism
b)   ☐ ecological validity
c)   ☐ gender bias
d)   ☐ xenophobia

7   *Numerical data can be described as:*

a)   ☐ qualitative
b)   ☐ quantitative
c)   ☐ psychometric
d)   ☐ projective

Answers: 1. a, 2. c, 3. b, 4. b, 5. c, 6. a, 7. b

Test your knowledge

Answer the multiple choice questions below by ticking the correct answer(s) to test your knowledge of methods. You will find the answers at the bottom of the page.

1 A lab experiment takes a research participant out of their natural environment. This causes a problem of:

a) ☐ reliability
b) ☐ validity
c) ☐ ethics
d) ☐ ecological validity

2 The case study method is often carried out on one individual. This means that the results lack:

a) ☐ ethics
b) ☐ reliability
c) ☐ generalisability
d) ☐ validity

3 When observers become part of the group they are observing, this is called:

a) ☐ non-participant observation
b) ☐ participant observation
c) ☐ inter-observer reliability
d) ☐ a case study

4 The problem with conducting a field experiment is that it is difficult to control:

a) ☐ extraneous variables
b) ☐ situational variables
c) ☐ participant variables
d) ☐ all of the above

5 Questionnaires and surveys are a type of:

a) ☐ observation
b) ☐ experiment
c) ☐ self-report
d) ☐ interview

6 If people are swayed by the opinions of others in giving their answers in a questionnaire, they may be showing:

a) ☐ social desirability bias
b) ☐ demand characteristics
c) ☐ gender bias
d) ☐ yea-saying

7 If an observer records behaviour every 20 seconds, this is an example of:

a) ☐ event sampling
b) ☐ time sampling
c) ☐ coding
d) ☐ observation

Answers: 1. d, 2. c, 3. b, 4. d, 5. c, 6. a, 7. b

Comparisons of approaches

Use the questions below to help consolidate your understanding of the approaches, perspectives, methods, issues and debates in psychology. Pages 292–309 of your textbook will help with this activity.

1 Compare the physiological approach with any one other approach/perspective.

   Hint: You may find it easier to choose an approach that is very different – for example, the social approach.

2 Compare the cognitive approach with any one other approach/perspective.

   Hint: Why not contrast with the behaviourist perspective, using treatment for phobias as an example?

3 Compare the individual differences approach with any one other approach/perspective.

   Hint: This is very different from the physiological approach.

4 Compare the developmental approach with any one other approach/perspective.

   Hint: This might link well with the cognitive approach in the development of children's thinking.

5 Compare the social approach with any one other approach/perspective.

   Hint: The social approach could be compared with the individual differences approach.

6 Compare the behaviourist perspective with any one other approach/perspective.

   Hint: You could contrast this with the psychodynamic perspective.

7 Compare the psychodynamic perspective with any one other approach/perspective.

   Hint: Why not choose the developmental approach?

8 Compare longitudinal with snapshot studies.

   Hint: Think about two studies you could compare.

9 Compare studies giving situational and individual explanations of behaviour.

   Hint: There is an emphasis on situational factors in the study by Geer and Maisel on control and stress reactions.

ExamCafé

Approaches, perspectives, methods, issues and debates

What the exam looks like

Sample approaches, perspectives, methods, issues and debates questions in Section B

1. (a) Using your knowledge of psychology, outline the design of a case study. (4)

   (b) Describe how the case study method was used in any two pieces of psychological research that you have studied. (8)

   (c) Using examples, compare the use of case studies with any one other method used in psychology. (12)

   (d) Explain the limitations of using the case study method. (8)

   (e) Discuss how the case study method can be useful in explaining human behaviour. (8)

2. (a) Using your knowledge of psychology, briefly outline the individual differences approach. (4)

   (b) Describe two pieces of psychological research that use the individual differences approach. (8)

   (c) Using examples of research that you have studied, discuss the strengths and limitations of explaining behaviour using the individual differences approach. (12)

   (d) Compare the individual differences approach with any one other approach in psychology. (8)

   (e) Discuss how the individual differences approach can be used in the nature–nurture debate. (8)

Exam question

1. (a) Using your knowledge of psychology, outline the design of a case study. (4)

Candidate's answer

A case study is a detailed description of a single person or small group of people under study or having treatment for a problem behaviour.

Examiner's comments:

This is a full enough answer to gain full credit. The candidate does not need to give examples for this question if they show understanding and have used psychological terminology.

Exam question

(b) Describe how the case study method was used in any two pieces of psychological research that you have studied. (8)

Candidate's answer

The case study method was used by Sigmund Freud in his analysis of a phobia of a five-year-old boy called Little Hans. Freud conducted his study through correspondence and interview with the boy's father and the reports cover a period of several years. The father gave Freud details of the boy's phobia of horses and of conversations he had with Hans. The problem of his fear of horses was analysed by both Freud and the father. Freud decided that the phobia was a result of his fear of losing his mother and his repressed longing for her and that horses were a representation of his father. Many of the examples of Hans's conversations and fantasies supported this explanation rather than a more common sense one that his fear may have been a result of seeing a horse fall down in the street. This case study like many other others is a detailed description of conversations and behaviour of one individual over a period of time.

Likewise, Thigpen and Cleckley conducted a case study of Eve White over a period of 14 months, in which time they recorded details of interviews with her in which she displayed symptoms of multiple personality disorder. Like the case of Little Hans, the researcher is the therapist who is conducting research into an individual for the purposes of therapy. However, in the case of Eve, the therapists used psychometric tests, projective tests and hypnosis not only to reveal the other personalities of Eve Black and Jane but to prove their existence.

Examiner's comments:

It is quite likely that candidates will use case studies from their AS course as they have learned these in great detail. This is perfectly acceptable in this question as long as they relate their answer to the case study method. This candidate has managed to pick out details from the studies that relate to methodology and has given a detailed, coherent, well-structured answer.

Exam question

(c) Using examples, compare the use of case studies with any one other
method used in psychology. (12)

Candidate's answer

The case study method differs from the experimental method in many ways. A laboratory experiment often has many variables under experimental control. For example, in the study by Dement and Kleitman on sleep and dreams, the participants are always woken by a doorbell and none of them allowed caffeine or alcohol before going to sleep. However, in the case study of Eve White, the therapist has very little control over the appearance of the other personalities and has to rely on using hypnosis to bring them out.

However, there are also similarities between case studies and experiments. Sometimes a case study is carried out under controlled conditions as in the case of the treatment of a nine-year-old girl for noise phobia by McGrath. Through a series of controlled sessions, the little girl was taught relaxation techniques and then was exposed to increasingly loud noises. It was the control over the volume and nature of the noise through a sequence of therapy sessions that enabled the girl to overcome her phobia.

Experiments, however, always seem to take place in a snapshot session and do not show behaviour over a period of time. For example, in the case of Pennington and Hastie, who investigated story order effects on whether or not a guilty verdict is given in court, the study only took one hour and so could be considered snapshot. However, in the case study of McGrath, the girl was treated over a number of weeks and her progress recorded as a longitudinal study.

Case studies and experiments may appear to have very little in common but in fact they both share the ability to provide useful applications to everyday life and in particular to therapists. Without the research of psychologists such as Budzynski into biofeedback and tension headaches under controlled conditions, therapists would not be convinced of its effectiveness. Likewise the case study of Eve White shows other therapists a way of resolving the personalities in multiple personality disorder as in the end Jane was the dominant personality and the others disappeared.

Examiner's comments:

This is a good answer with effective use of examples from the AS and A2 specification. Five is a good number of studies to refer to and shows that the student is able to apply the principles of research methods across different parts of the course. It also shows that the student has an impressive knowledge of a wide range of psychological evidence. The student has pointed out two similarities and two differences, which is sufficient for a top band mark.

Exam question

(d) Explain the limitations of using the case study method. (8)

Candidate's answer

The case study method has a number of limitations. One of the main problems is the close relationship that develops between the therapist and his client/patient. For example, in Freud's analysis of Little Hans his father questions him in order to support the theory of the Oedipus Complex. In the leading questions that the father asks his son, it would be easy to be biased in the interpretation of the responses. Little Hans's father rejects the more common sense explanation for his son's phobia and assumes that his son thinks the horse is symbolic of him.

Another limitation of the case study method is the amount of qualitative data that is collected, making it very difficult to analyse and interpret. In the case of Eve White, interviews over a period of 14 months were collected with a wealth of detailed data much of which would not shed any light on the problem of the different personalities.

Finally, case studies could be considered to be unethical if the therapist is making use of the client to develop his own theories. In the case of Thigpen and Cleckley this might be true as many people doubt the existence of multiple personality disorder.

Examiner's comments:

The student has raised a good number of limitations – two would be sufficient, three is very good – and has supported these points with a good range of examples. The detail in the examples is accurate, clear and well elaborated. The structure of the answer is good and psychological terminology used comprehensively.

Exam question

(e) Discuss how the case study method can be useful in explaining human behaviour. (8)

Candidate's answer

Case studies are useful because they show how psychological functioning can be understood in relation to family dynamics and trauma. Many of Freud's cases involved one-to-one discussions with his patients to reveal the causes of their anxiety. In the case of Little Hans it is not quite so clear how the questioning by his father helped to resolve his phobia but an attempt was made to resolve his anxieties and Freud claims many successes with individual cases.

Eve White came to the therapists with symptoms of headaches and blackouts. These distressing aspects of her behaviour were explained to her by the therapists as an aspect of her multiple personality disorder. Without this explanation, Eve White could not understand why she was suffering from these symptoms. The therapy sessions were useful to her and achieved her cure.

The problem with the case study in explaining human behaviour is that it is difficult to generalise to the wider population as it is often focused on one individual. Often the cases studied in therapy present unusual problems and hence the findings are not useful in explaining human behaviour in general. In the case of Little Hans, his phobia may have been caused by fear of his father but other cases of phobia may have had different causes and so this is not such a useful method to explain human behaviour.

Examiner's comments:

At this point in the examination some candidates will be running out of time and rush their points or not elaborate fully on their examples. This is not evident in this student's work as the answer is focused on the question and raises a good number of discussion points.

Your answers to a similar question

1. (a) Using your knowledge of psychology, outline the design of a laboratory experiment. (4)

   (b) Describe how the laboratory experiment method was used in any two pieces of psychological research that you have studied. (8)

   (c) Using examples, compare the use of laboratory experiments with any one other method used in psychology. (12)

   (d) Explain the limitations of using the experimental method. (8)

   (e) Discuss how the experimental method can be useful in explaining human behaviour. (8)

Candidate B answers

Exam question

2. (a) Using your knowledge of psychology, briefly outline the individual differences approach. (4)

Candidate's answer

This approach emphasises the uniqueness of the individual.

Examiner's comments:

Although accurate, this answer is a bit brief and requires further elaboration to explain the approach.

Exam question

(b) Describe two pieces of psychological research that use the individual differences approach. (8)

Candidate's answer

In his 16 personality factor questionnaire, Cattell is focusing on individual differences by giving each person a different personality profile. He is not looking for similarities between people but highlighting the differences between them. He is making the assumption that unique, inborn aspects of the individual influence all their behaviour.

Another piece of research that uses the individual differences approach is the case study of Eve White and the description of her multiple personality disorder. The study emphasises her particular personality differences without reference to other cases. It provides a detailed analysis of her three personalities and highlights the unique features of her problem.

Examiner's comments:

This answer is accurate and focuses on the question. The research is well chosen in the context of this study. However, the student has given limited details of the evidence and this could have been more fully elaborated.

Exam question

(c) Using examples of research that you have studied, discuss the strengths and limitations of explaining behaviour using the individual differences approach. (12)

Candidate's answer

One advantage of the individual differences approach to explain behaviour is that the research often focuses on a detailed description of one individual and hence a wealth of rich data is recorded and analysed. For example, in the case of Little Hans, Freud and the boy's father recorded details of conversations and fantasies over a period of several years.

However, a disadvantage of the individual differences approach is that it is difficult to generalise findings from one individual to the wider population. This is certainly true in the case of Eve White, who suffered multiple personality disorder with three personalities, and because the condition is uncommon it might be difficult to relate this to other cases.

Another advantage of the individual differences approach is, where psychometric tests are used to measure traits such as extroversion, the scores are quantitative and measured objectively. Tests such as these can show definitive differences between the personalities of athletes in different sports.

However, a disadvantage of the individual differences approach is that it could be considered reductionist to explain the behaviour of an individual by their personality profile. According to Cox, 2000, personality is only one of a number of factors that can contribute to athletic success.

Examiner's comments:

The student has identified two strengths and two weaknesses of the individual differences approach. The points discussed are appropriate and supported by relevant research but, as in the other answers from this student, the details of the evidence are a little sparse. The issue of reductionism could have been explained more fully and the example given was particularly brief.

Exam question

(d) Compare the individual differences approach with any one other approach in psychology. (8)

Candidate's answer

Compared to the social psychology approach, the individual differences approach could be considered quite ethical. Many studies in social psychology are unethical because they involve the manipulation of variables. For example, Milgram's participants thought they were administering an electric shock to the learner and this was very distressing for them. However, in the individual differences study of Eve White, although she became distressed because of her condition, this distress was not caused by the therapist. In fact, he was trying to help her.

On the other hand, many social psychology studies are done on large numbers of participants and so can be generalised. For example, Milgram used 40 participants in his study of obedience. However, Thigpen and Cleckley drew their conclusions about multiple personality disorder from studying one individual, Eve. This means that conclusions cannot be drawn about the disorder in others.

Examiner's comments:

It is disappointing that this student uses examples from the AS course without bringing in material from the A2 course in this answer. Credit will be given in this synoptic paper to research from the AS course, but to get full credit the range of material used should be broader.

Exam question

(e) Discuss how the individual differences approach can be used in the nature–nurture debate. (8)

Candidate's answer

The nature–nurture debate is a debate between biological determinants of behaviour and explanations of behaviour in terms of experience. The individual differences approach tends to favour the nature side of the nature–nurture debate. This is because studies like Kroll and Crenshaw show that athletes in different sports tend to have different personality profiles. There was a noticeable difference between team sports and individual sports, which suggests that personality determines which sport you will choose.

Examiner's comments:

This answer is a bit limited and it may be because the student has come to the end of the paper and has not left himself enough time to finish properly. Students should practise their essays with a time limit so they get used to the length of each section. One example is not enough for an eight-mark question no matter how well it is explained.

Your answers to a similar question

2. (a) Using your knowledge of psychology, briefly outline the physiological approach. (4)

    (b) Describe two pieces of psychological research that used the physiological approach. (8)

    (c) Using examples of research that you have studied, discuss the strengths and limitations of explaining behaviour using the physiological approach. (12)

    (d) Compare the physiological approach with any one other approach used in psychology. (8)

    (e) Discuss how the physiological approach can be used in the determinism vs freewill debate. (8)

Conclusion

Top ten tips for the exam

1. Ensure that your class notes are in order; it might be helpful to use dividers to separate your notes on each unit.

2. It is a good idea to keep testing yourself to see what you can remember and then to make a note of those points that you are struggling to remember, so that you can go over them and then test yourself again.

3. Try out a range of revision techniques to see which is most effective for you. (See the introduction of this book for ideas on how to revise effectively.)

4. Make sure you are familiar with the exam paper layout and that you carefully read not only the assessment questions but the instructions as well. This will ensure that your response includes everything that it should.

5. Take note of the total marks for each part of the question. This will help you decide how long you should spend on each part of the overall question.

6. Do plenty of practice exam questions. This is not only useful in terms of checking your knowledge, but it will also allow you to check your timing. You must ensure that you can write a full response in the time allocated.

7. If you are concerned that you may forget information when you get into the exam, then it is a good idea to write any information down – for example, psychologists' names, concepts, and so on – as soon as you are given permission to write in the exam, before you read the question.

8. Make sure that you plan your answer before you write it, particularly for those questions which are worth the greatest amount of marks.

9. Once you have completed your answers, it is worth taking the time to read over them again, to see if you can develop them further and to check for any errors or points that you may have missed.

10. Once you have finished the exam and have left the exam venue, try not to think about the answers you have given. Be confident that if you have put in the hard work during your AS and A2 years and you have revised effectively by following the tips and activities in this book, then you should be successful.

Answers to 20 Questions

Unit 3

Forensic Psychology (page 12)

1 Sutherland believed that criminal behaviour could be learned through communication, through personal groups, by learning criminal attitudes, because laws are deemed to be pointless and through association with criminals.

2 Should Heinz steal the drug that would cure his wife, but which he couldn't afford?

3 The enzyme MAOA (monoamine oxidase A)

4 Composites of external features were more easily identified than composites of internal features. External composites were also sorted at the same level as whole composites.

5 Interview similarity, focused retrieval, extensive retrieval and witness-compatible questioning

6 Canter concluded that rather than there being a distinction between two types of crime scenes in serial killings, all such crimes had an organised element.

7 Duffy lived in the area Canter predicted, his occupation was correct, and meant that he had some knowledge of the railway, he was the same age as Canter's prediction and he had been married.

8 Witness order

9 Students were asked whether they thought Mr Radford was guilty, and the photographs of 'Mr Radford' had previously been rated as attractive on a scale of 1–9.

10 Three hundred college students from an introductory psychology class, 150 male and 150 female, mostly white middle class

11 Orientation period, open confrontation, reconciliation

12 A stooge is an actor working with the researcher. In Nemeth and Wachtler's study, the stooge had to sit at the head of the table for the deliberation.

13 Offenders on conditional release in community-based employment schemes were less likely to return to custody and more likely to remain on conditional release than unemployed offenders.

14 Suggested improvements included: using prisons sparingly, less crowded prisons, decompression programmes to gradually reduce the effects of the prison environment and more assessments related to prison rather than life outside.

15 Participants thought that their probation officer would sort out their problems and were there for them to talk to. Probation officers were seen as independent and could offer advice on a range of topics.

16 Restorative justice involves the offender being encouraged to accept responsibility for their actions and be reintegrated into the community.

17 Sherman and Strang found restorative justice effective for perpetrators of violent crimes and property crimes.

18 Cognitive skills programmes are aimed at breaking down faulty thinking patterns which underlie criminal behaviour.

19 Cann believed that women offend for different reasons from men, so they did not necessarily have the cognitive skills deficits found in male offenders.

20 Self-reports from the prisoners and staff

Health and Clinical Psychology (page 30)

1 Perceived threat (seriousness and susceptibility), cues to action (internal and external) demographic variables, cost-benefits analysis

2 Internal and external

3 Questionnaires and number of chip-pan fires reported

4 Strong fear, medium fear, low fear and control

5 GHb (glycohaemoglobin) levels

6 Behaviourist

7 Twenty-four workers at a Swedish sawmill, fourteen finishers and ten cleaners/maintenance workers

8 A repeated design using the Hassles Rating, Hopkins Symptom Checklist and Bradburn Morale Scale every month for nine months and the Life Events Scale at the end of ten months

9 Photos of dead car crash victims

10 Death of a spouse

11 Identification of thoughts in stressful situations, coping strategies, putting strategies into real-life stressful situations

12 Participants with biofeedback showed fewer headaches, less muscle tension, lower hypochondriasis levels and less drug usage. After six months there was a reduction in symptoms such as depression, insomnia, apathy and fear of crowds. After 18 months there were still fewer headaches in the biofeedback group.

13 Prospective study

14 *DSM-IV* is a multi-axial tool for looking at disorders, which considers physical condition, social and environmental problems and overall functioning level. *ICD-10* is a criteria-based diagnostic tool.

15 Statistical infrequency, deviation from social norms, failure to function adequately, deviation from ideal mental health

16 They changed the gender in case studies of patients before giving them to clinical psychologists to see if diagnosis changed depending on the gender of the 'patient'.

17 Watson and Raynor used Little Albert to install a phobia through classical conditioning. They paired a white rat with a loud noise which frightened Albert, who very quickly acquired a phobia of the rat that he had not previously shown.

18 How often both twins show the same characteristics (in Gottesman and Shields's study, this was schizophrenia)

19 Rational emotive therapy, where activating events are identified, beliefs are then challenged and the consequences are considered (ABC)

20 Anxiety disorders leave a continuous feeling of fear which disables daily living, and can be triggered by seemingly trivial stimuli. Affective disorders are characterised by disabling moods which prevent normal life. Psychotic disorders involve a loss of contact with reality, and may include delusions, hallucinations and withdrawal from the outside world.

Sport and Exercise Psychology (page 49)

1 Warmth, reasoning, emotional stability, dominance, liveliness, rule consciousness, social boldness, sensitivity, vigilance, abstractedness, privateness, apprehension, openness to change, self-reliance, perfectionism, tension

2 There are significant differences in the personalities in different sports (except football and wrestling).

3 Social and environmental cues can cause aggression, particularly in heightened arousal situations such as sport.

4 Achievement motivation

5 Key terms were identified from literature and 32 identified by raters as representative of sporting achievement. These were tested on undergraduates twice to ensure reliability and then on high school students and were found to consistently differentiate between sports-orientated students and non-sports-orientated students – and the SOQ was formed.

6 Mice

7 Electrocortical, autonomic and behavioural

8 The SCAT (sport competition anxiety test) has 15 items relating to anxiety, which respondents rate as 'hardly ever', 'sometimes' or 'often'.

9 A sudden and dramatic collapse in performance due to the level of stress becoming too high

10 Vicarious experience, verbal persuasion, emotional arousal

11 Forming, storming, norming, performing, adjourning

12 By asking participants to clap and cheer in pairs, fours and sixes to see if performance levels altered with larger groups

13 A change in performance brought about by the presence of others

14 Non-coacting audience in a maze and in a run, and co-acting cockroach in a maze and in a run. In the run (a simple task) the co-acting cockroaches performed best; in the maze (a complex task) the co-acting cockroaches ran more slowly.

15 Home advantage is more pronounced in indoor sports; it leads to more offensive play; away disadvantage is often as significant as home advantage.

16 One to three hours of exercise a week could reduce breast cancer in women by 30 per cent; four hours a week raised this to 50 per cent.

17 Aerobic exercise group, weight-training group and stretch/flexibility control group

18 Rowing

19 Lower levels of training do not disadvantage athletes and may actually benefit them.

20 Participants were told that they were taking a new rapid-action oral anabolic steroid.

Psychology of Education (page 67)

1 Sensorimotor, pre-operational, concrete operational and formal operational

2 Cognitive development is influenced by interaction with others, using language.

3 They suggested that learning occurs as a result of association – classical conditioning.

4 Ways of organising information and ways of representing information

5 Seven: linguistic, logical-mathematical, spatial, musical, bodily-kinesthetic, interpersonal, intrapersonal

6 Remembering, understanding, applying, evaluating, creating

7 A curriculum in which subject matter is matched to the learner's cognitive level

8 When basic needs such as the need for food and safety are not met, learners are not motivated to meet their cognitive needs.

9 Children with good play experiences (High/Scope) showed better educational and social behaviour.

10 Attainment scores, interviewing teachers and policy makers and observation of classes

11 Learned helplessness means giving up after continually failing. If learners regularly fail in education they will give up trying.

12 Entity view and incremental view

13 Speaking out is effective in reducing bullying, and anti-bullying programming needs to focus on specific types of bullying.

14 It can show the types of communication between teachers and learners which can affect learning.

15 Teachers can: provide more than one context for using knowledge, use examples, provide more time, ensure learners have mastered one problem before moving on, use regular assessment and get students to think about their own learning strategies.

16 One-to-one or small-group tutoring for 30 minutes each day for up to 20 weeks, using multi-sensory techniques for sounds and word formation, and adult support in reading and comprehending stories

17 Stages of fluency: new to English, becoming familiar with English, becoming a confident user of English, fully fluent in English. Background measures: age, gender, SEN, FSM, ethnic group, time spent in Key Stage 2 school, prior attainment

18 Raising aspirations by taking students on educational trips, bringing in consultants, and projects emphasising options on leaving school

19 Pre-school girls have better communication, social and cognitive skills. During Foundation to Key Stage 3 girls do better at English and slightly better at maths. At Key Stage 4 girls out-perform boys, particularly in humanities, arts and languages. At A level girls do better in most subjects but there is less of a gap than previously.

20 Using interactive activities that were short and focused; using speaking and listening to support writing; teacher creativity; using ICT; realistic targets; mentoring; team-building initiatives; involving disengaged boys in projects; raising self-esteem by paired reading; using befrienders; committed staff; single sex lessons.

Stretch and Challenge

To stretch yourself you can go beyond the required information that is detailed in the specification, and research additional evidence for some (or all) of the topics you have covered. For example, in Health and Clinical Psychology there is the opportunity to look at biological treatments in addition to the drug therapy researched in the evidence in the specification. These could include ECT, psychosurgery or genetic modification. You could also look at other disorders such as post-traumatic stress syndrome, in addition to phobias as an anxiety disorder.

If you look at general psychology books on the topics you are studying, you are likely to find that there is more evidence which you could use to extend your knowledge. If you are researching on the Internet, look at refining your research, for example by using Google Scholar rather than simply Google.

To challenge yourself you need to make links between different topics, such as topics from your AS studies. For example, linking phobias to Freud's study on Little Hans will give a different explanation from the psychodynamic perspective and will be in addition to the three approaches/perspectives covered in the specification. Your conclusion about these, related to the exam question, can show sophisticated analytical skills which are required in a high-grade answer.

Suggested reading

Forensic Psychology

Dwyer, D. (2001) *Angles on Criminal Psychology*. Cheltenham: Nelson Thornes

Canter, D. (2008) *Criminal Psychology: Topics in Applied Psychology*. London: Hodder Arnold

Health and Clinical Psychology

Sarafino, E. (2008) *Health Psychology: Biopsychosocial Interactions* (6th edition). New York: John Wiley and Sons

Davison, G.C. and Neale, J.M. (1982), *Abnormal Psychology: An Experimental Clinical Approach*. New York: John Wiley and Sons

Sport and Exercise Psychology

Cox. R.H. (2002) *Sport Psychology: Concepts and Applications* (5th edition). New York: McGraw-Hill

Weinberg, R. and Gould, D. (2006) *Foundations of Sport and Exercise Psychology*. Leeds: Human Kinetics

Psychology of Education

Fontana, D. (1995) *Psychology for Teachers (Psychology for Professional Groups)*. Basingstoke: Palgrave Macmillan

Lefrancois, G.R. (1999) *Psychology for Teaching (Education)*. Belmont, California: Wadsworth Publishing